THE ART OF ENTERTAINING
RELAIS & CHATEAUX

Menus, Flowers, Tablesettings, and More for Memorable Celebrations

RELAIS & CHATEAUX NORTH AMERICA AND JESSICA KERWIN JENKINS
INTRODUCTION BY PATRICK O'CONNELL
PHOTOGRAPHY BY MELANIE ACEVEDO AND DAVID ENGELHARDT

RIZZOLI NEW YORK

New York · Paris · London · Milan

TABLE OF CONTENTS

INTRODUCTION

For the first time, some of the world's greatest authorities on entertaining share their secrets to hosting spectacular parties and events. • Since every Relais & Châteaux property in North America offers its own unique ambiance, you will no doubt be inspired by the range of imagination and creativity. Each member's special style and the personality of its owner are reflected in the types of events featured—from a rustic farm picnic to a Gilded Age-inspired New Year's Eve celebration. • Visiting a Relais & Châteaux often feels like being an invited guest at a fabulous house party from a bygone era. Thoughtful and creative touches abound. For these events everything has been carefully considered to create an indelible memory. Studying the efforts of these experts one can better understand the importance of advance planning and the correct marriage of food and surroundings as well as the key ingredients of fun and whimsy. • Join us as we celebrate life's most memorable moments. May the work of these passionate hosts inspire you to view the art of entertaining from a fresh perspective and deepen your appreciation for the art of living joyfully.

Patrick O'Connell

Chef Proprietor
The Inn at Little Washington
President, Relais & Châteaux North America

Afternoon TEA

RESPECTING TRADITION, AFTERNOON TEA SERVED IN THE
CHARMING GARDENS OF THE CHARLOTTE INN IS A GRAND RITUAL, FULL OF
DAINTY DELICACIES DISPLAYED ON GRACEFUL SERVICE.

Assortment of Teas   Kayo Manhattan   *Gravlax Tea Sandwiches*
Cucumber Tea Sandwiches   *Deviled Eggs with Osetra Caviar*

* RECIPE PROVIDED

T here are few hours in life more agreeable," Henry James once declared in *The Portrait of a Lady*, "than the hour dedicated to the ceremony known as afternoon tea." And there are few places more agreeable in which to sip a good cup of tea than in the lush, wondrous gardens of The Charlotte Inn in Edgartown, Martha's Vineyard.

Early in the nineteenth century, one of Queen Victoria's ladies-in-waiting, Anna Maria Stanhope, 7th Duchess of Bedford, invented the tradition of afternoon tea by inviting friends to her boudoir for a midday snack in order to stave off hunger when her late-night dinner was still hours away. For the duchess, tea and cakes perfectly cured the "sinking feeling" she experienced at five o'clock, but it also gave her guests a chance to sit back and relax and to catch up with the latest gossip.

Certainly Stanhope would have approved of the delectable way in which tea is laid out in The Charlotte Inn's pretty gardens with their flowers in bloom, gracefully rambling pathways, and fascinating antiques. "We take an elevated approach to everyday life," says the inn's executive chef, Justin Melnick, "and little details make all the difference."

An island landmark since the 1930s, the once-neglected inn—buckets catching rain in the hallway during the off season—was brought back to life by Gery Conover and his wife, Paula, in 1972. The inn's original owner, Charlotte Pent—*the* Charlotte—had just as much determination. She converted the family's grocery store to a hotel and met local skepticism with a "familiar twinkle in her eye," the local paper reported in 1934. But the property, set in the heart of Edgartown, the first colonial settlement in Martha's Vineyard, quickly became an institution. Its quaintness and its sophistication are perfectly suited to its environment in a seaport village showcasing stately Greek Revival houses and surrounded by quiet harbors, beaches, and rolling sheep farms.

Just as the fabled Charlotte did, Gery and Paula have made the inn their home, and their golden retrievers, Barclay and Nicky, are known to one and all. For over forty years, with dedication the duo has cleverly created an ambiance that blends tradition and wit, punctuated

The meandering and intimate gardens showcase Gery and Paula Conover's array of curious European antiques—from Parisian planting boxes to iron urns once installed at an English manor house. The seating is arranged in cozy roomlike settings that encourage conversation. A table laid with Limoges tea service and antique hotel silver sets a civilized tone for afternoon tea (see previous spread) as demure roses climb the iron gates and fill a sterling bud vase.

by an enviable and vast collection of antiques tucked into every nook of the inn's four mid-nineteenth-century buildings—cut-glass decanters, rotary dial phones, riding boots, leather hat boxes, and aristocratic family crests. (Carly Simon, James Taylor, and Billy Joel have all enjoyed Room 14's baby grand piano.)

"Even though the decor is Edwardian, it's definitely not stuffy," Paula explains. "It's elegant, but we try not to take everything too seriously." In the library, parakeets flutter in an antique French brass birdcage. In an upstairs hallway, a collection of forty vintage flashlights is displayed in a mahogany cabinet. The lower level of the Coach House is full of antique ice skates and letter sweaters, tennis rackets and wooden skis, while the Conovers' famous brass and wood letterbox collection hangs on a wall in the dining room. At teatime, guests in the garden are served on Limoges china, while signature cocktails and homebrewed iced tea sparkle in glasses selected from the Conovers' collection of antique stemware.

"There's nothing like the good old stuff," says Paula, "the porcelain tubs and the antique doorknobs. People do notice all the details." (Of course, when the Conovers bought a vintage one-thousand-pound porcelain tub for Room 17, installing it in the old inn required a three-week rebuild of the bathroom floor and six men to maneuver the piece into place.) Still, on their frequent antiquing trips to London, Boston, or New York, Paula is the one who knows when to leave an antique treasure behind. Gery has a harder time walking away. "Sometimes I do have to remind him that you can't dance with every pretty girl," Paula says with a laugh.

Their passion for bygone glamour extends outdoors. They have brought their discriminating eye to the gardens, cultivating an intimacy that invites guests to gather on comfortable wicker settees. Planter boxes once graced an old Parisian café. Antique terra-cotta tiles lining the meandering brick pathways were found on a Newport estate. Blooming with rhododendrons and clematis, the gardens are overhung with fifty-year-old wisteria and the scent of roses. The sound of a splashing antique fountain soothes from the distance.

In eighteenth-century England, tea gardens like this one were where the aristocracy went to relax—that is, until too many rakes took advantage of the hidden bowers. At the inn, however, the delights are culinary in nature. In keeping with the grand English tradition, Melnick serves cucumber finger sandwiches on Pullman bread, layered with cream cheese and sprigs of fresh dill. "We like to set out something a little on the lighter side, something refreshing," he says. And guests who linger long enough might try the chef's bracing Kayo Manhattan, made with bitters and rye.

The table is set with crisp Frette napkins and fresh garden roses. Everything is utterly simple, and just so. "There is so much care put into every aspect," Melnick explains. The chef's house-cured gravlax, for example, is ordered directly from Alaska, traveling from Alaskan dock to the inn's back door within twenty-four hours. Lending classic deviled eggs a luxe twist, Melnick uses house-made aioli and a little sustainably harvested caviar. "It's the attention to detail," he says, "the subtle little touches that make all the difference. You could take short cuts, but we do things the right way."

KAYO MANHATTAN

The Charlotte Inn's chef, Justin Melnick, named this bracing cocktail after his grandfather, William Kayo. It features WhistlePig Rye, and is still a favorite at Melnick family gatherings.

MAKES 1 COCKTAIL

4½ ounces WhistlePig Rye
Splash of sweet vermouth
2 dashes of Angostura Bitters
3 brandied cherries, plus 1 teaspoon cherry juice

Pour the rye and vermouth into a shaker full of ice. Add the bitters and cherry juice. Stir to chill and slightly melt the ice. Strain into a chilled martini glass and garnish with the cherries.

GRAVLAX TEA SANDWICHES

When one is creating any recipe, the quality of the ingredients is the most important factor. The inn has its salmon flown in overnight from Alaska, fresh out of the water. While that cannot always be done in the home setting, finding a good, trustworthy fish market will often do the trick. The salmon cures for three days—so plan accordingly.

MAKES 6 TO 8 SERVINGS

Gravlax
1 (1½- to 2-pound) side salmon, skin on, deboned
Juice of ½ lemon
2 tablespoons Pernod Ricard
¾ cup firmly packed light brown sugar
¾ cup kosher salt
1 tablespoon whole black peppercorns
4 fresh dill sprigs, roughly chopped

Tea Sandwiches
1 loaf brioche bread (white bread can be substituted)
1 small container crème fraîche
Snipped fresh chives

For the gravlax: Place the salmon, skin side down, on a large piece of cheesecloth on a perforated pan. Set the pan inside another pan to catch the drippings. Drizzle the lemon juice and Pernod over the fish evenly.

In a bowl, combine the brown sugar, salt, peppercorns, and dill, creating the curing mixture. Completely cover the salmon with the curing mixture, using more on the thicker end and less on the thinner tail portion. Wrap the overhanging cheesecloth over the fish and place a weight on to press. Place in the refrigerator and cure for three full days.

Wipe off any excess curing mixture and thinly slice.

For the sandwiches: Preheat the oven to 350°F.

Using a bread knife, cut the brioche loaf into slices that are about ½ inch thick. Cut out rounds with a 2-inch round cookie cutter and place on a baking sheet. Toast in the oven until golden brown, 3 to 5 minutes.

Assemble the tea sandwiches by spreading the crème fraîche in a thin layer on the toasted brioche rounds. Place thinly sliced salmon over the crème fraîche and garnish with chives. Serve on a large platter or individually plated.

HOW TO
SERVE TEA

—

In times gone by, when tea was still scarce in England, the mistress of the house kept her tea caddy locked, spooning it out to guests herself and, occasionally, washing and drying her precious tea set personally—with a dainty tea towel and much ceremony. There was a customary way to stir the tea noiselessly, and conventions dictated how to maneuver a lemon slice and how to pour. Though drinking tea is now an everyday luxury, the pleasure of serving it with ritual and just a hint of pomp remains.

Properly brewed, tea should never be made with water that has been left to simmer or with twice-boiled water, and the more quickly the water is heated, the better the tea. (Evaporation leads to a higher mineral content, or harder, more bitter water.) Additionally, a porcelain teapot can be pre-heated by swishing and draining a bit of hot water through it before brewing tea.

Naturally, steeping time and the quantity of loose tea added can change the strength of the brew. Typically three minutes is a suitable steep time. One of the most popular black teas at The Charlotte Inn is Wedgwood Original Tea, a classic, blending tea from India and Kenya.

Afternoon tea isn't a meal in the proper sense, but it creates a delicious pause between lunch and dinner, one that lends guests time to catch up with friends while enjoying a few savory bites.

CUCUMBER TEA SANDWICHES

The Charlotte Inn's very simple recipe is a nice refreshing summer treat, especially as cucumbers start coming out of the garden, still warm from the sunshine.

MAKES 6 TO 8 SERVINGS

8 slices fresh white bread
Cream cheese
2 to 4 cucumbers (depending on size), peeled and thinly sliced
Olive oil
Sea salt
Chopped fresh dill

Spread an even layer of cream cheese on 4 slices of the bread. Shingle the cucumber slices over the cream cheese, covering completely. Drizzle olive oil over the cucumbers and sprinkle with sea salt to taste. Sprinkle with fresh dill and place the remaining 4 slices of bread on top to form sandwiches.

Trim the crusts from the sandwiches, creating perfect squares. Place a skewer or toothpick in each quadrant and quarter each sandwich by slicing through the centers. Serve on a larger platter or individually plated.

DEVILED EGGS
WITH OSETRA CAVIAR

This is The Charlotte Inn's take on a very classic dish, elevated with the use of Osetra caviar.

MAKES 6 TO 8 SERVINGS

6 large farm-fresh eggs
2 to 3 tablespoons Aioli (below)
Worcestershire sauce
Kosher salt and freshly ground black pepper
Osetra caviar
Snipped fresh chives and thinly sliced pickled shallots
    for garnish (optional)

Place the eggs in a saucepan of cold salted water and bring to a boil. Once the water begins to boil, turn to medium heat and simmer for exactly 9 minutes. Immediately cool the eggs by running cold water into the pot. Peel the eggs when cool.

Cut the eggs in half lengthwise, remove the yolks, and set the whites aside. Blend the yolks with the aioli and a dash of Worcestershire sauce in a stand mixer with the paddle attachment or with a handheld mixer, then season with salt and pepper.

Spoon the yolk filling into a pastry bag fitted with a fluted tip. Season the cooked egg white halves with salt and pepper and place, cut side up, on a large serving platter. Pipe the filling into the cavity of each egg white. Spoon the caviar into the center of each egg half and garnish with chives and pickled shallots (if using).

Aioli
The aioli will keep in the refrigerator for up to 1 week. Use leftovers as you would commercial mayonnaise.

MAKES ABOUT 1 CUP

1 large egg yolk
1 tablespoon Dijon mustard
1 teaspoon finely minced shallot
Fresh lemon juice
1 cup canola oil

In a large bowl, combine the egg yolk, mustard, shallot, and a squeeze of lemon juice and whisk until combined. While continuously whisking, slowly drizzle in the canola oil in a steady stream, being careful to keep the emulsion. Incorporate all the oil and taste for seasoning. You may need to add some water to gain the right consistency.

Note: Place a rolled-up, wet towel beneath the bowl like a nest to keep it from moving as you whisk.

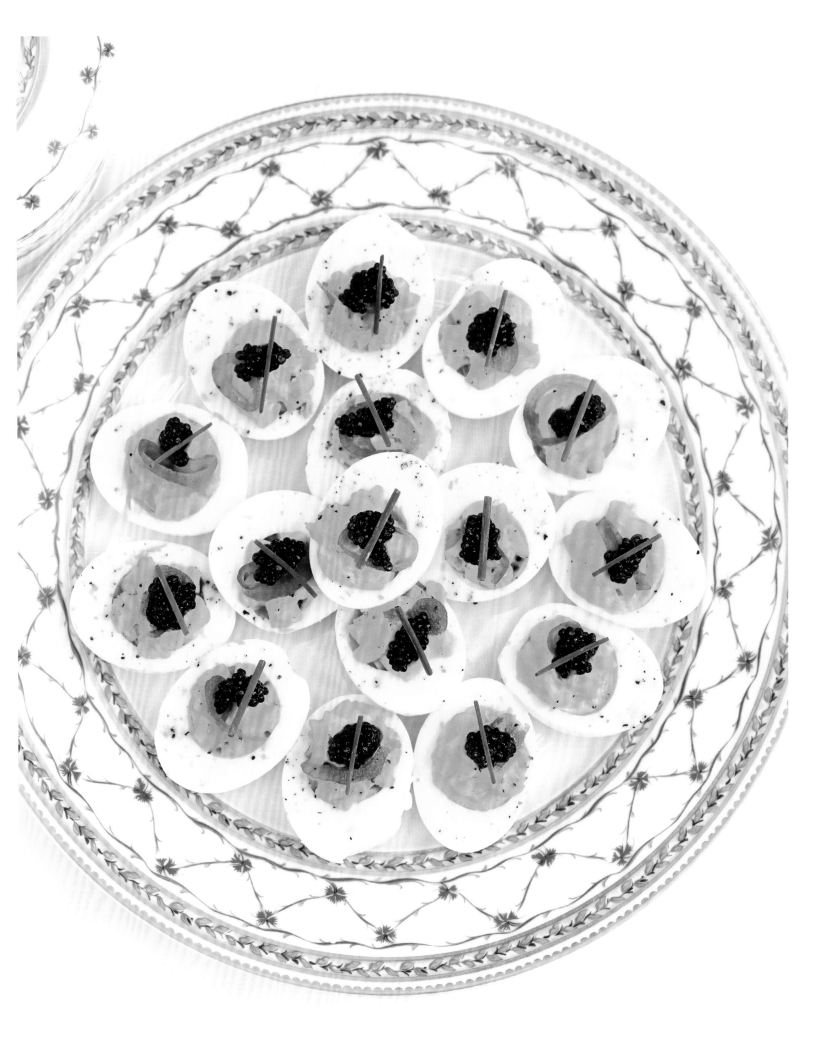

THE INN AT DOS BRISAS

WASHINGTON, TEXAS

Wildflower CELEBRATION

UNDER THE WIDE TEXAS SKY, A RUSTIC AND REFINED DINNER CELEBRATES THE BIG, BOLD TASTES OF CLASSIC COWBOY COOKERY—ELEGANTLY MODERNIZED—AND THE SPRAWLING FIELDS OF SPRINGTIME'S FRAGRANT FLOWERS.

*Dos Brisas Strawberry Martini** *The Garden Cocktail* *Espresso Chicken** *Beef Bourguignon**
*Honey-Braised Collard Greens with Swiss Chard and Green Cabbage** *Marinated Kohlrabi**

* RECIPE PROVIDED

Thereʼs nothing like Texas in the springtime, when the rains transform its barren terrain with wildflowers that burst riotously into bloom. In March and April, full fields of brilliantly vivid blossoms stretch toward the horizon, and the roadside is carpeted with Indian paintbrush, phlox, and—most beloved of all—bluebonnets. For Texans, no other flower "brings such upsurging of the spirit and at the same time such restfulness," local folklorist J. Frank Dobie once said. "The evanescences of petal and leaf mingling into an aroma that is at once delicate and as tonic as a heiferʼs breath." Itʼs just that blend of rousing and rustic that defines Dos Brisasʼs unique charm. A stay at the ultra-luxe ranch revives all the senses, and never more so than during wildflower season, when guests might dine alfresco in the midst of all the big, bold natural glory.

At Dos Brisas, in the eastern foothills of the fabled Texas Hill Country, much has remained unchanged since the nineteenth century, when cotton farmers, horse trainers, and cattlemen passed through. Enter through the stately gates and drive more than a mile and a half before reaching the inn itself, through horse pastures, fields, and gardens. Hundreds of the 313 acres are left unmowed and unspoiled. Two winds cool the property—the dos brisas, or "two breezes" that arrive from the southwest and the north each day, contributing to the easy, breezy atmosphere. (Though, as proprietor Doug Bosch, tells it, the name was also chosen because his initials were already emblazoned on the propertyʼs iron gates.)

A reverential nostalgia and love of the outdoors enchants every corner, and is inflected with classically Texan largesse. In one of three fishing ponds, you might catch bass, sun perch, or catfish—any of which can be cooked up for dinner. Thereʼs a clay range for shooting in the afternoon. Guests toss horseshoes, eat sʼmores, and take hayrides. Riding the trails beside a meandering creek lined with ancient oak trees, one finds tiebacks in every picnic-perfect little knoll along the banks.

Serene and sensational, wherever guests wander, Dos Brisasʼs verdant landscape blooms in springtime—both in the garden and in its vivid fields of wildflowers. As seen in the previous spread, simple glass jars filled with buds and displayed alongside old-fashioned brass lanterns on a dark wooden table runner set the lighthearted tone. In order to retain each dishʼs heat long after itʼs left the cookstove, and after the evening sun has gone down, Dos Brisas serves the meal in individual cast-iron crocks.

The heart of Dos Brisas is its forty-two-acre certified organic farm, adjacent to the kitchen. The staff harvests daily in order to create its exquisitely seasonal dishes. The farm itself decides the menu. Similarly, wine director Thomas Perez has both a seven-thousand-bottle cellar that includes some of Europe's most exciting wines at his disposal and, when creating his exciting seasonal cocktails, all that the farm has to offer. Walking through the gardens he dreams up signature drinks like a strawberry martini, using tiny organic berries grown on site, or The Garden, a Waterloo gin–based cocktail blending several varieties of heirloom peppers with grapefruit and lime, and garnished with a sprig of cilantro. For guests who fall for his concoctions, or who long to express culinary creativity of their own, there are farm tours, mixology lessons, and cooking classes that celebrate both heirloom vegetables and five-star cuisine.

Every spring, however, the ranch's renowned dinners among the fields of wildflowers, offer a unique perspective on the Dos Brisas experience. A horse-drawn carriage pulled by Sampson, a handsome Clydesdale, ferries friends from their Spanish-style haciendas out to the edge of a picturesque meadow where an elegant table is laid, right down to its burnished silver napkin rings, and where the chef prepares meals on an open fire.

Since the state was founded, back when cowboys ruled the land, Texans have been cooking over campfire cauldrons filled with hot wood ash. But unlike the cowboy chuck wagon of yore, the Dos Brisas pantry overflows with deliciously fresh selections from the garden. The chef starts by spit-roasting an espresso-rubbed rotisserie chicken stuffed with cut herbs—thyme, rosemary, lemon balm, and sage—which allows the precious, fragrant cooking juices to infuse the dishes bubbling below. Collard greens slowly braise in a clay pot with Swiss chard and green cabbage, all seasoned with white wine vinegar, more herbs, local honey, and a squeeze of lemon, while an earthy kohlrabi marinated in olive oil, rosemary, and thyme slow roasts over the smoky hardwood fire. The pièce de résistance, however, is the beef bourguignon, which simmers for hours in a cast-iron cowboy cauldron over the wood flames as wisps of smoke float above the pot, offering their particular flavor to the classically French dish.

This scene offers a quintessential taste of Old Texas that is informed by today's gracious good living. It's a true spectacle, with the robust scent of the fire and the wildflowers brightening the meadows all the way to the horizon. What a breathtakingly delicious way to usher in the spring.

Dos Brisas's garden of delights, encompassing forty-two acres of organic heirloom vegetables and herbs, supplies a bounty to the kitchen, including onions for the slow-cooked beef bourguignon and tiny strawberries used in signature drinks like the strawberry martini. Additionally, the ranch offers classic Texan thrills for young and old such as hayrides, fishing, archery, and clay shooting. Riding trails wind through all the prettiest pastures and lead to the most idyllic picnicking spots, including a creek overarched with ancient oaks and tieback posts at the ready.

At the edge of civilization, creative forethought emphasizes the simple pleasures of dining alfresco, with a cozy, comfortable table setting using hay-bale benches covered with lengths of linen. Soft linen napkins banded with silver rings offer an elegant contrast to the natural surroundings, while nothing in the tabletop's neutral palette detracts from the awe-inspiring views. A rustic planked bar, like the one seen here, offers the perfect serving solution when dining is far from the kitchen and can be constructed using wooden fencing built into three portable, easy-to-store panels.

DOS BRISAS
STRAWBERRY MARTINI

Strawberry shortcake in a glass.

MAKES 1 COCKTAIL

6 fresh strawberries
Tahitian vanilla bean
Dash of simple syrup (one part sugar, one part water)
2 ounces Tito's Handmade Vodka
¼ ounce fresh lime juice
Splash of club soda

In a cocktail shaker, muddle the strawberries and vanilla bean with the simple syrup. Add the vodka, lime juice, club soda, and ice and gently shake. Strain into a martini glass.

ESPRESSO CHICKEN

Cowboys and coffee 'round a fire in Texas: The Inn at Dos Brisas marries the two American classics—chicken and coffee—by rubbing a whole chicken with espresso powder, then slowly roasting the bird above glowing wood embers, to create a wonderfully burnished chicken and a heartwarming dish.

MAKES 6 TO 8 SERVINGS

2 (2- to 2½-pound) whole organic chickens
1 teaspoon kosher salt
1 teaspoon freshly ground white pepper
3 sprigs each fresh thyme, rosemary, lemon balm, and sage
1 tablespoon high-quality espresso beans, ground
1 garlic clove, minced

Start a fire of oak and pecan wood early in the pit of a cowboy grill. Let the flames die down to glowing embers covered in ash.

Blot the chicken dry of any moisture and season the surface and cavity with the salt and white pepper. Fill the cavity with the thyme, rosemary, lemon balm, and sage. Using a 12-inch length of kitchen string, truss the chicken, keeping the legs and wings tight to the body. Liberally rub the espresso powder and garlic on the surface of the chicken, making sure no area is left uncovered.

Skewer the chicken on a motorized rotisserie spit, securing it so that it will rotate without spinning around the skewer. Place the spit about 6 inches over the glowing wood embers, set the rotation for slow to medium speed, and cook until the chicken is cooked through and a thermometer inserted into the thigh portion of the chicken registers 165°F; this should take 1 to 1¼ hours, depending on the heat of the coals.

Carefully remove the cooked chicken from the spit and allow it to rest for 10 minutes before carving it into 8 pieces.

BEEF BOURGUIGNON

Texas is renowned for its beef and for its hearty dishes. The inn takes the classic French red wine–infused beef stew and makes it their own by slow cooking prime Wagyu beef, apple wood bacon, and pearl onions, ensuring a buttery texture and complex flavors.

MAKES 6 TO 8 SERVINGS

3 pounds Wagyu beef short plate, cut into 1-inch cubes
Kosher salt and freshly ground black pepper
1 cup all-purpose flour
3 tablespoons unsalted butter
½ pound apple wood slab bacon, diced
3 tablespoons grape seed oil
1 garlic clove, chopped
5 medium onions, cut into medium dice
3 carrots, cut into medium dice
½ cup tomato paste
1 (750-milliliter) bottle red table wine, preferably red Burgundy
30 pearl onions, peeled
Sachet of 1 fresh thyme sprig, 1 bay leaf, and 3 whole black peppercorns
2 quarts veal or beef stock

Preheat the oven to 250°F.

Blot the beef of any moisture and season liberally with salt and pepper. Dredge the beef in the flour and tap off the excess. Place on a clean tray and reserve.

Melt the butter in a Dutch oven over medium-high heat. Add the bacon and sweat until browned and most of the fat is rendered. Remove the bacon and reserve.

Add the grape seed oil to the pot and heat through. In batches, add the beef and brown on all sides. Remove the beef and reserve.

Add the garlic, onions, and carrots to the pot and sauté until translucent. Add the tomato paste and cook, stirring, until lightly caramelized. Add the red wine and simmer for a few minutes to evaporate the alcohol. Return the beef and bacon to the pot, along with the pearl onions, sachet, and stock. Bring to a boil, then reduce to a simmer.

Cover the pot and transfer to the oven. (You can also cook on the stove top at a very low simmer.) Cook for 2 to 3 hours, until the beef is fork tender. Discard the sachet before serving.

HONEY-BRAISED COLLARD GREENS WITH SWISS CHARD AND GREEN CABBAGE

Cool, blustery spring evenings in Texas are a perfect match for anything braised. The inn combines the Southern staple collard greens with Swiss chard and cabbage for a hearty side that stands up to rotisserie chicken.

MAKES 6 TO 8 SERVINGS

1 large bunch collard greens
1 large bunch Swiss chard
1 head green cabbage
4 slices thick-cut bacon
1/2 cup (1 stick) unsalted butter
1/4 cup Champagne vinegar
2 tablespoons local honey
3 fresh thyme sprigs
1 bay leaf
Kosher salt and freshly ground black pepper
1 lemon, halved

Wash the collard greens thoroughly. Remove the tough stems that run down the center of each leaf by holding a leaf in your left hand and stripping the leaf away with your right hand. The tender young leaves in the heart of the collards don't need to be stripped. Stack 6 to 8 leaves on top of one another, roll up, and slice into 1/2- to 1-inch-thick slices.

Wash the Swiss chard thoroughly and use the same method to remove the tough stems. Roll up the leaves and slice into 1/2-inch-thick slices.

Cut the cabbage into quarters and remove the center spine. Thinly slice each quarter into 1/4-inch-thick slices.

In a heavy skillet over medium heat, slowly sweat the bacon in the butter until it begins to brown. Add the collards, vinegar, honey, thyme, and bay leaf. Cover and cook for 35 to 40 minutes. Add the chard and cabbage and continue to cook for 15 to 20 minutes longer, until all the greens are tender. Season with salt and pepper, then finish with a touch of lemon juice. Discard the thyme sprigs and bay leaf and serve.

MARINATED KOHLRABI

With hearty dishes comes the need for a hearty vegetable. The inn marinates kohlrabi for 24 hours, then slow roasts this cabbage cousin to lose the bite and become wonderfully inviting.

MAKES 6 TO 8 SERVINGS

1/4 cup extra virgin olive oil
1 fresh thyme sprig
1 fresh rosemary sprig
1 teaspoon fleur de sel (sea salt)
6 whole kohlrabi, leaves intact

Combine the olive oil, thyme, rosemary, and salt in a bowl.

Remove the outer leaves and stalks of the kohlrabi. Liberally coat the kohlrabi with about 3 tablespoons of the olive oil marinade. Reserve the remaining marinade. Cover the kohlrabi and refrigerate for 24 hours.

Place the kohlrabi on the grill at the side of the roasting Espresso Chicken (page 30). Grill the kohlrabi, turning often to maintain even browning, until fork tender, 20 to 30 minutes, depending on the size. Remove from the grill and let rest for 5 minutes. Slice into medallions and drizzle each serving with some of the remaining marinade.

Fourth of July BEACH BALL

WITH STARS AND STRIPES (AND SPARKS A-FLYING), TRADITIONAL AMERICAN FARE, AND LOADS OF SUMMERTIME FUN, OCEAN HOUSE HOSTS A ROLLICKING CROWD ON THE BEACHFRONT FOR THIS PATRIOTIC HOLIDAY.

*Flavored Popcorns   Canapés   Mini Hot Dogs with Assorted Condiments   Root Beer–Glazed Pulled Pork**
Apple and Jicama Coleslaw   Country Potato Salad   Summer Vegetable Ratatouille**

* RECIPE PROVIDED

Ocean House, known in its late nineteenth-century heyday as the "Queen of Atlantic resorts," reigns once more over a particularly romantic stretch of Rhode Island's rugged coastline. Everything about the place is regal, from the sweeping ocean views to a top-to-bottom reconstruction, which took five years and cost investors $147 million. It's only right that, in honoring the hotel's legacy, every year in planning the eagerly anticipated Beach Ball chef John Kolesar creates a bang-up, star-spangled menu to match.

The hotel's original structure, built in 1886, was one of the few local establishments to survive the devastating Long Island Express, a hurricane that wiped out much of the competition in 1938. Instead, time and neglect took their toll. Some upper floors were condemned and the rest were deemed a fire hazard when the well-loved institution finally closed in 2002. In order to save the hallowed place, it was razed to the ground. A meticulous architectural re-creation followed, returning some five thousand rescued artifacts to their former glory and including a painstaking rehabilitation of the central fireplace, which was dismantled and then reassembled stone by stone. Now, the old chandeliers sparkle. The antiquated mahogany and bronze elevator cab is housed inside a modern one. The concierge stands behind the hotel's original reception desk. The martini glasses are narrow and deep. With utter accuracy, architects and designers have delivered the very essence of old-world glamour.

But then, the reason one comes to Ocean House is not solely to revel in the details, but to get out into the great outdoors. "The winds, from whatever direction, bring the cool, bracing sea air," a late nineteenth-century visitor to Watch Hill noted. "The temperature in summer never oppresses." The powerful poignancy of the hotel's surroundings, perched on a bluff jutting out into Block Island Sound, simply invite awe, and the wide, elegant veranda beckons, just as it did back in 1916, when it made a perfect backdrop for the silent film American Aristocracy, starring Douglas Fairbanks in a bow tie and straw boater, and playing a nebbish entomologist in hot pursuit of a pretty socialite, elbowing his way into "Narraport" society.

By steamboat, horse and carriage, and later by train, at the end of the nineteenth century

Monumental in every way, Ocean House, set on a cliff overlooking the sea, is as dramatic as it is charming. Its every detail ferries visitors back in time. On the Fourth of July, guests make their way through the tumbling beach roses along the elevated boardwalk and are greeted with holiday fanfare, including a fife and drum band (see following spread). Star-spangled bunting makes a perfect table runner, while silver buckets full of hydrangeas and ribbon-tied votive candles keep the tablescape bright, crisp, and clean.

and into the twentieth, well-heeled visitors flocked to Watch Hill, each family favoring one of a handful of neighboring resorts. In those days, guests amused themselves with lawn parties and rounds of croquet (still a favorite pastime). Daily baseball games were held in one of Ocean House's fields, while a hillside near the sidelines made a very comfortable grandstand for devotees. Children rode the "flying" horses of a carousel left behind by a traveling carnival. The clientele was prestigious, but unpretentious. "The young girls dress with perfect simplicity in dainty gingham and outing flannels, rather than in the overelaborate raiment at Newport," as one late nineteenth-century writer pointed out.

It was, another vacationer remembered, "the best of all possible worlds, with the big hotels the center of so much activity—balls, cotillions, whists, concerts, lectures; with fierce competition between them for having the finest orchestra, the jolliest crowd, the most delicious food, the best baseball team." Members of the younger set made the rounds, showing off their savvy by performing the latest dance steps. And today, just as in those days when Ocean House was known perennially to host the most brilliant ball of the season, the management knows how to throw a good party.

Every Fourth of July on the hotel's private white-sand beach, bordered by wild rose brambles and lanky marsh grass, the chaises and umbrellas are cleared away and out comes the dance floor. "We like to have fun. In inspiration, it's a backyard party," says Kolesar, who serves up plenty of standards, from potato salad to summer ratatouille. "But we've taken it to a different level." Don't let the simple table settings and modest red-white-and-blue bunting fool you. An old-school popcorn machine serves up lobster-flavored popcorn, then a batch seasoned with duck fat and goat cheese, or truffle and Parmesan. A tray of canapés displays intriguing push-up tubes, each housing the ingredients of an impeccable tuna tartare. The hot dog cart is stocked with mini three-inch dogs, custom ordered from a Vermont smokehouse, and condiments include foie gras mayo. "I like to take the new, fun ingredients and make them approachable," says Kolesar. This chef has plenty of tricks up his sleeve.

Last summer, his favorite moment of the evening was watching guests' jaws drop as servers marched in with a whole roasted pig. "An Ocean House event is successful because we create a buzz, a theater," says Kolesar. "Guests love the show." They also loved the seven-foot-high tiered dessert stand displaying four thousand individual cupcakes, macaroons, and tiny gâteaux, and timed to arrive just as a fifteen-minute fireworks spectacle began to erupt from the hotel's barge out on the bay. (It's only fitting that Ocean House's celebrations should sail a bit over the top. This is a place that once lured the likes of Henry Ford, Clark Gable, and Frank Sinatra, after all.) Then, it's over in an instant, with eight months of work igniting in the thrill of the moment.

Still, every November, long after the band's stopped playing and the happy crowds have dispersed, Kolesar begins anew, dreaming and scheming, plotting out inventive ways that his team can best themselves come July. "I don't know how we will outdo last year's party," he says with a contented sigh, "but we will try like hell to exceed ourselves once again."

ROOT BEER–GLAZED PULLED PORK

To get the most succulent meat for Ocean House's pulled pork, chef John Kolesar employs a signature dry rub before smoking the pork shoulder—low and slow—for five hours, sealing in the flavor and juices. Combined with a root beer–spiked house-made barbecue sauce, the result is pure porky perfection.

MAKES 8 SERVINGS

Ribs

1 (8-pound) pork shoulder
2 tablespoons molasses
1 cup Dry Rub (right)
3 cups apple wood chips

Barbecue Sauce

MAKES ABOUT 8 CUPS

3 tablespoons vegetable oil
2 cups diced Spanish onions
2 jalapeño chiles, seeded and diced
4 cups Yacht Club Root Beer
6 cups ketchup
1 cup apple cider vinegar
2 cups Dry Rub (right)
2 cups firmly packed dark brown sugar
1 cup molasses

For the ribs: Rub the shoulder with the molasses and then the dry rub and refrigerate for about 1 hour.

Soak the apple wood chips in water for about 40 minutes. Set up your smoker for indirect heat at 250°F. Place the soaked wood chips in the smoker.

Place the shoulder in the smoker and smoke for about 5 hours, until the meat pulls apart and is tender.

Meanwhile, for the barbecue sauce: In a large stockpot, heat the vegetable oil over medium heat. Add the onions and sweat until translucent, 10 minutes. Add the diced jalapeños and sauté for an additional 5 minutes. Deglaze with the root beer, bring to a simmer, and cook until the liquid is reduced by half. Add the ketchup and cider vinegar and whisk until everything is incorporated. Add the dry rub, brown sugar, and molasses. Puree in the pot with a handheld blender. Cook over low heat for about 20 minutes. Let cool.

To serve: Pull apart the meat and slather individual servings with the barbecue sauce.

Dry Rub

MAKES 3 CUPS

3/4 cup smoked paprika
1/2 cup firmly packed dark brown sugar
1/4 cup ground espresso
1/4 cup kosher salt
1/4 cup freshly ground black pepper
1/4 cup granulated garlic
1/4 cup onion powder
1/4 cup chili powder
2 tablespoons ground cumin
2 tablespoons cayenne pepper
2 tablespoons Chinese five-spice powder
2 tablespoons ground cinnamon

In a small bowl, mix together the paprika, brown sugar, espresso, salt, black pepper, garlic, onion powder, chili powder, cumin, cayenne, five-spice powder, and cinnamon.

COUNTRY POTATO SALAD

Potato salad is an all-American side found at every summertime barbecue. For Ocean House's Fourth of July Beach Ball, fresh ingredients are mixed with simple flavors to create the perfect accompaniment to the smoky pulled pork.

MAKES 8 SERVINGS

4 strips North Country Smokehouse Applewood Bacon
2 pounds small red potatoes, unpeeled
Kosher salt and freshly ground black pepper
1/2 cup mayonnaise
2 teaspoons whole grain mustard
4 dashes of Tabasco sauce
1 scallion, thinly sliced
1/4 cup diced celery
3 large eggs, hard-boiled, peeled, and chopped

Cook the bacon until crispy. Drain, reserving a few tablespoons of the grease. Crumble the bacon and set aside.

Place the potatoes in a large saucepan and cover with cold water. Add 1 tablespoon of the bacon grease and some salt. Bring to a boil over medium-high heat and cook until the potatoes are tender, 15 to 20 minutes. Drain and let the potatoes cool. Cut into bite-size pieces and place in a large bowl.

In a separate bowl, mix together the mayonnaise, mustard, Tabasco, and salt and pepper for the dressing.

Toss the dressing with the potatoes, scallion, celery, and eggs. Add the bacon. Cover with plastic wrap and refrigerate until chilled before serving.

SUMMER VEGETABLE RATATOUILLE

Summer vegetables in New England are some of the best in the country and perfect to complement Ocean House's rich barbecue fare. With bold greens and yellows, their summer-edition ratatouille looks as good as it tastes.

MAKES 4 TO 6 SERVINGS

2 cups fresh fava beans removed from the pods
1 pound yellow wax beans
1 pound haricots verts
2 zucchini
2 yellow squashes
2 ears of fresh corn on the cob, unshucked
1 tablespoon vegetable oil
1 red onion, diced
8 garlic cloves, smashed
1 cup dry white wine
3 tablespoons unsalted butter, cubed
2 teaspoons kosher salt
1 teaspoon freshly ground black pepper

Fava beans have a waxy outer coating that needs to be removed. Blanch them in boiling water for 30 seconds, then transfer with a spider or slotted spoon to an ice bath to stop the cooking process. Peel off the waxy coating and set the beans aside.

Clip off each end of the yellow beans and haricots verts. Blanch the beans in the simmering water for about 6 minutes, until tender. Shock in an ice bath to cool. Set aside.

Cut the zucchini and yellow squashes lengthwise into quarters and remove the seeds. Shuck the corn and remove the silk. Remove the kernels from the cobs.

In a large sauté pan, heat the vegetable oil over medium-high heat. Add the red onion and garlic and sauté until translucent. Deglaze with the white wine. Add the butter, fava beans, yellow beans, haricots verts, zucchini, squashes, and corn. Season with salt and pepper, and cook for an additional 10 minutes, until heated through and the flavors have blended. Serve hot.

Serving miniaturized hot dogs looks great on the plate and gives guests the chance to try all the delectable condiments and combinations. At Ocean House, chef John Kolesar sent out three-inch hot dogs alongside mustard, ketchup, homemade relish, sauerkraut, and roasted red pepper jam, as well as foie gras mayonnaise. "I like to take the new, fun ingredients and make them approachable," he explains.

Olmsted Garden
LONG TABLE LUNCH

IN THE FABLED GARDENS—ENVISIONED BY THE LEGENDARY NINETEENTH-CENTURY OLMSTED FAMILY—CHEF JASON BANGERTER SERVES A LONG, LINGERING LUNCH OF FANTASTICALLY FRESH SUMMERTIME DELIGHTS.

Langdon Lemonade*   Beet Negroni*   Peter Rabbit Margarita*   Trout Mousseline en Fleur de Courgette*
Langdon Hall Heritage Hen with Mushrooms and Hen Bone Cream*

* RECIPE PROVIDED

Whether taking in the artful mix of flowers in Langdon Hall's Cloister Garden, the wisteria-smothered pergola, the sweeping lawns laid out in the bucolic manner of the eighteenth-century English picturesque school, or the deep woods surrounding it, the artful views offered by the storied inn always leave guests longing for more.

Perfectly restored, it's easy to imagine the satisfaction this idyllic spot brought to Pauline and Eugene Langdon Wilks, great-grandson to New York's preeminent Gilded Age baron John Jacob Astor. Their twenty-five-thousand-square-foot summer home was built in 1902 with imposing Federal-style majesty, and boasts a grand symmetry, stately ionic columns, and views of the silvery Grand River on a forty-acre property that stayed in the family until 1982. After several years, it was purchased by the current owners, Canadian architect and developer William Bennett and his business partner and wife, Mary Beaton, and turned into a distinctive inn.

Yet, while the house's original molding and trim and paneling are intact, and antique chairs that were once found in Astor's house on Lafayette Square in New York City (now Astor Place) grace the rooms, "the Victorian gardens, which had been renowned, had all but disappeared," says Bennett. In the orchard, the ancient apple trees had not been pruned for decades. The cedar hedges were ravaged, the vegetable garden barren, save a lone stand of rhubarb.

Five years of intensive rejuvenation followed, headed by one of Canada's most esteemed garden historians, Dr. Leslie Laking, who made dozens of visits, poring over old landscape drawings, uncovering lost flower beds, and making an exhaustive inventory of every tree. Yet, it wasn't until ten years ago that Bennett and Beaton learned that the estate's revived gardens had been designed by John Charles Olmsted, partner in the great American landscape firm founded by his illustrious stepfather, Frederick Law Olmsted.

Langdon Hall Country House is rigorously classical, from its imposing edifice to the opulent gardens surrounding the house, planted as the famous Olmsted firm envisioned them at the beginning of the twentieth century. On the previous spread, Elaine Martin, the in-house floral designer, arranges roses picked that morning. On the following spread, Carole Precious, owner of a local farm, gathers eggs to serve at the inn, accompanied by her hen Sarah.

At first, when John Charles met the Wilkses in his office in 1902, he doubted whether they would ever become clients. But with their stellar home completed just that year, Pauline had grand plans. She'd just been hunting at the Vanderbilts' 250-room French château, Biltmore, in North Carolina, and yearned to emulate the vast, lush Olmsted gardens there. Her husband was less convinced, and was, in fact, "wholly satisfied" with Langdon Hall's gardens as envisioned by the "local talent," Olmsted noted. However, one can never underestimate the persuasive powers of a woman who "longs for more beauty," as Olmsted also astutely observed. Pauline wanted more, and, happily, on that hallowed day she—and beauty—conquered all.

Correspondence between the Wilkses and the Olmsted firm revealed the placement of terraces and wild grapes, honeysuckle, bayberry, and hydrangeas. Now, over one hundred years later, the rolling acres of restored Olmsted gardens at Langdon Hall remain a picturesque treasure. And the dappled shade of the well-loved and gnarled camperdown elm the Wilkses planted (to Olmsted's specifications) make a perfect spot to linger over a long, luxurious lunch, showcasing the glorious abundance of the property's enviable kitchen garden.

In Carolinian country, a warm corridor in southernmost Canada, north of Lake Erie and west of Lake Ontario, a surprising range of flora more often seen in the southern United States are found—magnolia, wild yam, black walnut, and sassafras. In the woods morel mushrooms appear in the fall and fiddlehead ferns in the spring. Water lilies float gently in the formal water garden, and Chinese geese parade past the main dining room, following along a winding grass path bordered by roses. Two ancient gray granite stone walls surround beds in the kitchen garden, restored on their original site.

A bumper crop of tomatoes hangs on the vine come summertime, just as in antique photos of the spot, and the kitchen garden's beds, laid out in the manner of an eighteenth-century French parterre, overflow with rare and delectable cultivars. "Early in the morning the mist sits just above the ground. I like to walk through the garden collecting samples of the items that are ready—new flowers blooming, little ripe vegetables hanging on the vine," says chef Jason Bangerter. "I take them back to the kitchen with thoughts of where they will be used in the day's menus."

At the height of the season, lunch in the garden demonstrates the full intensity of these fresh flavors, all showcased with more than a little Gilded Age opulence. The chef's menu is "simple and elegant, but with technique and a classical touch," and includes poached zucchini flowers filled with a delicate pillow of trout mousse. A sweet pea puree, served with the zucchini blossoms, comes right from the garden. "I love walking through the garden gate," he says. "Every time I do, I get excited—the intense aroma of herbs and flowers, the visual pleasure of the abundant organic bounty. It's a chef's dream." Heritage breed hens come from just down the road.

Apparently, however, lingering in the gardens at Langdon Hall is a dream shared by many. "It's funny," he adds. "No one ever wants to leave, and if you leave your seat, it's to get up and smell a flower. It's easy to sit there for three hours. It's like a fairy tale, beautiful and mysterious."

The table is set with early nineteenth-century English Spode china in a green-and-white leafy pattern perfectly suited to the garden, each plate numbered on the back by a workman. The flatware chosen for the occasion is of the same era and of similar provenance, manufactured in Sheffield, England, in the late nineteenth century and seen here in its original case. The floral arrangements combined some delicate flowers from the garden with roses from the Toronto flower market in tiny bud vases of cut glass.

BEET NEGRONI

The earthy and sweet notes from the beet cordial perfectly complement the herbal and bitter notes of a negroni.

MAKES 1 COCKTAIL

½ ounce beet cordial (see Note)
½ ounce The Botanist Islay Dry Gin
½ ounce sweet vermouth
Lime or lemon twist
Beet crudité (very thin slice of raw beet)

Fill a rocks glass with ice and add the beet cordial, gin, and vermouth. Garnish with a twist and beet crudité.

Note: To make a beet cordial, simmer chopped beets in a simple syrup (equal parts sugar and water) until the beets are soft. Strain and keep refrigerated.

PETER RABBIT MARGARITA

A green-thumb twist on the classic cocktail.

MAKES 1 COCKTAIL

1½ ounces Sauza Gold Tequila
½ ounce triple sec
1 ounce carrot juice
½ ounce fresh lemon juice
Spoonful of orange marmalade
Kosher salt
Ginger beer
Fresh rosemary sprig

In a cocktail shaker, shake the tequila, triple sec, carrot juice, lemon juice, and marmalade. Dip the rim of a cocktail glass in the salt and fill with ice cubes. Strain the cocktail and pour over the rocks, then top with ginger beer. Garnish with a rosemary sprig.

Langdon Lemonade To make Langdon Hall's singular lemonade (makes 2 quarts), strain 3 cups fresh lemon juice through a fine sieve into a pitcher. Add 2 cups superfine sugar and stir until dissolved. Stir in 4 cups water and some ice, then garnish with mint and lavender fresh from the garden.

TROUT MOUSSELINE EN FLEUR DE COURGETTE

Such a lovely, light starter for a hot summer day. Langdon Hall presents a delicate, elegant trout mousse wrapped in the flower of the zucchini plant. To serve, chef Jason Bangerter whips up a sweet pea puree that bursts with bright fresh flavors. Another suggestion is to shave raw baby zucchini, then toss with a simple vinaigrette to serve beside the flowers. Or simply garnish the plates with cured trout roe, crème fraîche, bronze fennel tops, pea vines, or peppery nasturtium flowers and leaves.

MAKES 6 SERVINGS

12 ounces boneless, skinless fresh Ontario lake trout fillet,
*   well chilled*
1 small egg white, well chilled
2/3 cup heavy cream (35 to 40 percent fat), well chilled
Kosher salt and freshly ground white pepper
6 zucchini flowers
Fish stock or water
Olive oil for brushing
Sweet Pea Puree (right)

Chill the bowl and blade of a food processor. Be sure the trout, egg white, and cream are very well chilled. Puree the trout in the bowl of the food processor until smooth. With the machine on, add the egg white and slowly add the cream in a thin stream, mixing until incorporated. Season with salt and white pepper. Transfer to a bowl, cover, and chill.

Gently open the flowers, revealing the bulbous stigma. Remove by pressing at the base inside the flower. It will snap off with a little pressure.

Spoon the trout mousse into the flowers (you can also use a piping bag). Close the flowers to form tiny barrel shapes. Chill for 1 hour.

Bring 4 inches of fish stock or lightly salted water to a light simmer in a saucepan. Add the stuffed flowers and gently simmer (be careful not to let boil), for 4 to 6 minutes, until the mousse is firm to the touch. (The cooking time will vary depending on the thickness of the rolled flower. After 4 minutes, unwrap one and slice to reveal the center; it should be a fully cooked pâté. If the center is still liquid, cook a minute or so longer.) Remove with a slotted spoon onto a paper towel and drain well. Brush with olive oil.

To plate: Spoon the puree onto 6 serving plates and top with a stuffed flower.

Sweet Pea Puree

In addition to serving as a herbaceous punch of garden flavors to accompany the zucchini flowers, this elegant puree is a terrific chilled light summer soup.

MAKES ABOUT 4 CUPS

1 tablespoon vegetable oil
1/2 cup sliced fennel
1 shallot, sliced
2 small garlic cloves, sliced
1/2 teaspoon minced fresh ginger
1/2 cup dry white wine
3 cups vegetable stock, fish stock, or water
3 cups fresh shucked peas
1 cup mixed fresh basil, mint, coriander, tarragon, parsley,
*   dill, and chervil leaves*
Kosher salt and freshly ground white pepper

Heat the vegetable oil in a saucepan over medium heat. Add the fennel, shallot, garlic, and ginger and sweat until tender and translucent. Deglaze the pan with the white wine, then reduce by two-thirds. Add the stock and simmer for 5 minutes. Add the fresh peas and continue to simmer for 4 minutes, until the peas are just cooked. Add the mixed herbs and remove from the heat. Season with salt and pepper. Let sit for 2 minutes. Strain, reserving the pea mixture and the cooking liquid.

Using a food processor, carefully puree the pea mixture in batches. Add some of the pea cooking liquid only as needed to create a smooth velvety texture.

Place a bowl large enough to hold the pea puree over another bowl of ice. Pass the puree through a fine sieve into the chilled bowl to cool quickly and retain the bright green color and flavor of the ingredients. Cover and store in the refrigerator until ready to use.

LANGDON HALL HERITAGE HEN
WITH MUSHROOMS AND HEN BONE CREAM

Langdon Hall is surrounded by an ancient Carolinian forest and some fantastic farmland, providing the kitchen with incredible ingredients. Relationships have been built with local farmers, foragers, and artisans who share the mission of providing wholesome natural products, prepared with care and respect. These producers' game birds and pure bloodline hens are some of the best in the area.

MAKES 2 SERVINGS

Chicken Jus
6 pounds chicken bones (carcass, necks, or wings),
  roughly chopped
2 tablespoons vegetable oil
2 cups roughly chopped carrots
2 cups roughly chopped leek whites
1 cup roughly chopped onions
1 cup mushroom stems and trimmings
1 cup dry white wine
4 quarts chicken stock or water
5 fresh thyme sprigs
8 fresh parsley sprigs
2 fresh bay leaves, cracked
10 whole black peppercorns
Kosher salt

Caramelized Shallot Puree
1 tablespoon vegetable oil
2 cups sliced shallots
1 cup heavy cream (35 percent fat)
2 tablespoons sherry vinegar
Kosher salt and freshly ground white pepper

Foraged Mushrooms and Swiss Chard
2 cups foraged mushrooms, such as chanterelles and morels
1 tablespoon unsalted butter
1 teaspoon minced shallot
1 teaspoon minced garlic
4 large rainbow Swiss chard leaves
½ cup chicken or mushroom stock
Kosher salt and freshly ground white pepper

Apricots
4 ripe apricots
1 tablespoon sugar
Kosher salt
Freshly ground grains of paradise
Leaves from 4 fresh lemon thyme sprigs

Hen Bone Cream
1 tablespoon vegetable oil
Bones and trimmings of 1 hen, roughly chopped
2 shallots, sliced
3 garlic cloves, sliced
½ cup mushroom stems and trimmings
½ cup Madeira or dry sherry
1 cup chicken stock
5 fresh thyme sprigs
1 fresh bay leaf, cracked
2 cups heavy cream (35 to 40 percent fat)
Kosher salt and freshly ground black pepper
Splash of truffle oil (optional)
Splash of lemon juice or Champagne vinegar (optional)

Chicken
1 tablespoon canola oil
2 bone-in, skin-on chicken breasts
Kosher salt and freshly ground black pepper
½ cup (1 stick) unsalted butter, diced
4 fresh thyme sprigs

For the chicken jus: Preheat the oven to 450°F.

Rinse the bones in cold running water. In a roasting pan large enough to hold the bones and vegetables, toss the bones with the vegetable oil and roast for 15 minutes in the oven. Stir in the carrots, leek whites, onions, and mushrooms. Roast for another 15 minutes, or until the bones are a rich golden brown and the vegetables are beginning to caramelize. Add the white wine to the pan to deglaze, then transfer the ingredients to a saucepan, using a rubber spatula to get all the drippings from the roasting pan.

Add the stock (enough to just cover the contents of the saucepan, about ½ inch above the bones). Bring to a simmer, and skim any impurities that rise to the surface. Add the thyme, parsley, bay leaves, and peppercorns and reduce the heat to a simmer. Continue to skim, cooking slowly, until the liquid is reduced to one-third of the original volume. Into a smaller saucepan, strain the sauce through a fine sieve to remove the solids. Discard the solids and continue to reduce the jus to the desired sauce consistency. Strain again through a fine sieve or cheesecloth into a bowl. Adjust the seasoning with salt.

For the shallot puree: Heat the vegetable oil in a saucepan over medium-high heat. Add the shallots and cook, stirring, until caramelized, about 15 minutes. Reduce the heat, add the cream and vinegar, and simmer for 8 minutes, until the shallots are tender and the cream is flavored. Drain, reserving the cream. Let the shallots cool slightly, then carefully puree in a food processor. Add enough of the reserved cream to the blender as needed to create a smooth velvety texture. Season with salt and white pepper.

For the mushrooms and chard: Clean the mushrooms of dirt, leaves, and twigs with a paring knife or a mushroom brush and trim the bottoms. Rinse the mushrooms thoroughly and dry on paper towels.

Melt the butter in a sauté pan over medium heat, add the mushrooms, and cook for 1 minute. Add the shallot, garlic, and chard leaves and cook a minute longer. Add the stock and bring to a simmer. Reduce until the mushrooms are glazed and the leaves are wilted. Season with salt and white pepper.

For the apricots: Heat the broiler to high, or have a kitchen torch handy.

Split the fruit in half and remove the pits. Season with the sugar, salt, and grains of paradise. Place in an ovenproof dish or skillet and broil or brûlée with the torch until the tops are caramelized. Sprinkle with the lemon thyme.

For the hen bone cream: Heat the vegetable oil in a saucepan over medium heat. Add the bones and trimmings, and sauté until golden brown. Add the shallots, garlic, and mushrooms to the pan. Reduce the heat and cook until tender. Deglaze the pan with the Madeira and cook down to a glaze. Add the stock, thyme, and bay leaf. Bring to a simmer and reduce the liquid by two-thirds. Add the cream. Bring the cream to a simmer and cook until the cream has taken on the flavor of the reduction and is the consistency of a smooth velvety sauce, about 8 minutes. Strain the sauce into a saucepan through a fine sieve and keep warm. Discard the solids.

Adjust the seasoning with salt, black pepper, and a splash of truffle oil, if you like. This sauce is quite rich and decadent. Add a splash of lemon juice or Champagne vinegar to balance acidity, if you wish.

For the chicken: In a large sauté pan, heat the canola oil over high heat. Season the breasts on both sides with salt and black pepper. Place the chicken, skin side down, in the oil and reduce the heat to medium-low. Cook until the fat of the skin is rendered and the skin is golden brown and crispy, 3 to 4 minutes. Turn onto the flesh side and add the butter and thyme. Cook, basting the chicken with the butter, until cooked through, about 10 minutes on each side. Remove from the heat and let rest for 3 minutes before serving.

To plate: Cut the chicken from the bones into thin slices. For each plate, spoon chicken jus onto the plate and top with 2 chicken slices. Add a quenelle of shallot puree, then the apricots and the mushrooms. Top with the hen bone cream.

THE KITCHEN GARDEN

The kitchen garden, established during an era when the staff sent its harvest by train to Langdon Hall's first owners in New York City, provides chef Jason Bangerter (seen striding through the beds on the facing page, top left) with an abundance of produce as well as inspiration. "The garden is the focus of the menu," he says. There he's discovered curious ingredients such as the 'Orange Gem' marigold (Tagetes tenuifolia), *which has a bright, citrusy flavor. He's been letting the garden decide the menu ever since. "I hadn't used marigold before coming here and it really changed my philosophy." Meanwhile, head gardener Mario Muniz relies on the marigold's ability to repel pests along the pathways and in the pesticide-free garden beds. "They make a beautiful border," says Muniz. Similarly, both chef and gardener enthuse about borage, with its bright marine-blue blooms that boast a cucumber-like flavor while providing essential pollen for the property's happily thriving bee colonies.*

Geranium is another planting that both Bangerter and Muniz rave about, especially the lemon-scented 'Minor' geranium (Pelargonium crispum), *and the orange-scented* Pelargonium, *'Orange Fizz'. "Geranium has a very citrusy and pungent taste," says Bangerter, who uses the plant's leaves when marinating wild salmon, juiced in a vinaigrette, or to flavor small loaves of bread. "You could make geranium ice cream or geranium sorbet or infuse the whipped cream for a cake with geranium," he says. "You could even dehydrate geranium leaves and dust their powder over a dessert."*

AUBERGE DU SOLEIL

RUTHERFORD, CALIFORNIA

Summer Sunset CELEBRATION

AS THE SUN SINKS BELOW NAPA VALLEY'S RIDGELINE, STUNNING SPARKLING WINES TWINKLE, THEIR BUBBLES CATCHING THE LAST LIGHT, AND GUESTS SAMPLE AN EFFERVESCENT ARRAY OF FLAVORS TO MATCH.

Selection of Sparkling Wines *Islay Negroni** *Raw Bar*
*Seared Diver Scallops with Zucchini, Corn, and Basil Puree** *Peach Parfaits**
Selection of Desserts, including Pâte de Fruits, Macarons, and Bon-Bons

* RECIPE PROVIDED

At its core, Napa Valley is all perfect pairings—rugged with romantic, laid-back with luxurious, and, of course, the right wine with the right food. But rarely is the subtle art of fusion demonstrated with such sophisticated savoir faire as at Auberge du Soleil, which first introduced the California-meets-France ethos to the valley. As visitors quickly realize, this particular cross-cultural connection is a match made in heaven—and sipping a glass of French champagne at sunset out on Auberge du Soleil's terrace overlooking the treelined ridge of the Rutherford Bench is nothing short of sublime.

Sparkling wine, like the valley itself, is a celebrated marvel of nature, one first discovered by the seventeenth-century French Benedictine monk Dom Pierre Pérignon, who oversaw the vineyard at his abbey. Traditionally, his wine had to be drunk before Easter, before it started to fizz, which was considered a flaw. Before long, however, Perignon learned to regulate the effervescence, and by the middle of the eighteenth century a suave supporter named Jean-Rémy Moët, of the great winemaking family, had introduced champagne to all the Parisian cognoscenti. It became a favorite among French kings, and the ladies of Versailles found the drink deliciously feminine. "Champagne is the only wine that leaves a woman beautiful after drinking it," noted the Marquise de Pompadour, a loyal customer. Peter the Great drank it nightly. Napoleon didn't imbibe often, but when he did he sipped champagne "to restore his strength and produce cheerfulness of spirit," according to his secretary.

Of course, scarcity didn't hurt the bubbly wine's glowing mystique. In those days champagne was still incredibly difficult—and dangerous—to produce and transport. Excessive bottle shattering, due to excessive froth, kept supplies low and demand high. In 1746, one poor winemaker managed to save only 120 bottles of the six thousand produced by his vineyard. Yet, not surprisingly, when supply met demand, the variety that frothed the most vigorously—called *saute-bouchon* (or "pop cork")—was the most expensive of all.

The outdoor terrace design used tendrils of passion vine and billows of white chiffon to embellish the trellis. Crystal chandeliers were suspended above an antique mirrored table surrounded by French carved pillar seats topped with linen cushions. On the tabletops, roses ruled, with arrangements blending yellow garden roses, soft peach 'Juilienne Roses', and blush Sahara roses, with a mix of white scabiosa, lisianthus, and green hydrangea.

The raw bar—offering oysters, Monterey Bay spot prawns, and razor clams—delivers the tangy taste of the sea. Chef Robert Curry resists the urge to overcomplicate things, letting the freshness of the seafood speak for itself. "When you eat an oyster—especially when paired with the effervescence of a sparkling wine—it is just so crisp and refreshing," he says. "It's all about simplicity and showing off the ingredients." The chef's other key ingredient is "plenty of ice."

Like those winemakers of the past, the adventurous California restaurateur Claude Rouas knows a thing or two about recognizing beauty and taking risks. If Napa was still something of a wild frontier in the late 1970s, his subtle infusion of French inspiration made it chic. Born and raised in Algeria, Rouas has a penchant for easy elegance, and began his career waiting tables at the ultra-posh Maxim's in Paris before opening his own boîte, L'Étoile, in Nob Hill, serving beluga caviar and champagne to San Francisco's jet set. When Rouas traveled to the valley and looked at sixteen acres on the east side of the Silverado trail, he saw Provence. Sure, it was a gamble, but Auberge du Soleil's opening brought the L'Étoile crowd out in force in 1981, and, with the addition of the inn several years later, decorated by Michael Taylor with plush furniture and in sandy hues, soon enough the place all but defined contemporary California style.

Auberge du Soleil's unique allure blends a sense of secluded tranquility and understatement with a fine-toned romance that hits its height as the sun goes down over the olive groves, vineyards, and mountains in the distance. Who could resist an invitation to come sip champagne there? "At sunset on the terrace, everything tastes better—there's just this sense of awe with that view," says executive chef Robert Curry.

At his raw bar, a carefully selected range of shellfish—oysters, Monterey Bay spot prawns, razor clams, and fresh urchin and crab salad—complements the exquisite champagnes being poured and heightens the rising sense of utter satisfaction. "The natural salinity of the ocean water, that freshness, is so perfect with sparkling wine," says Curry, who also served diver scallops sautéed right out on the deck and garnished with squash blossoms, Brentwood corn, and a basil puree.

"The whole idea is to bring out the best in the wine," he notes. On the classic side, there are potato-leek croquettes with Osetra caviar and lemon crème fraîche. More daring combinations include compressed Sharlyn melon, burrata, and mint as well as lobster and wakame tartlets with mango and basil.

In perfect Napa fashion, the chef is fastidiously local when crafting his menu and in selecting his provisions. "I've spent almost twenty-five years in the valley and it's all about relationships," he says. "My relationships to the people who are fishing and farming, and their relationship to the waters and the land." Napa was named "land of plenty" by the Wappo, the Native Americans who originally inhabited this valley. The bounty of the harvest is as stunning as the views of terrain.

And yet, on occasion, every chef yearns for more. Complementing the local flavors with an exotic taste of France gives it all thrilling depth. From Laurent-Perrier's Ultra Brut to Pommery's "wonderfully polished" Cuvée Louise to what wine director Kris Margerum calls the "crème de la crème," Moët & Chandon's Dom Perignon Rosé, that evening the corks flew, though he also saber-cut one bottle, just for good measure. (Keep the bottle super cold and strike the seam, he suggests.) As many guests noted, standing on the terrace, enjoying the vistas and the warm, soft air, the rosé perfectly reflected the evening's glowing rosy skyscape. It's pure magic when the sunset light catches bubbles.

SEARED DIVER SCALLOPS WITH ZUCCHINI, CORN, AND BASIL PUREE

Fresh zucchini, corn, and basil are summer staples that exemplify the bounty of the Napa Valley. Executive chef Robert Curry pairs these essential ingredients with naturally sweet scallops, offering a layered and flavorful taste of the season.

MAKES 8 SERVINGS

1 small zucchini
2 tablespoons grape seed oil
Kosher salt and freshly ground black pepper
2 ears of fresh white corn on the cob
6 tablespoons chicken stock
2½ tablespoons unsalted butter
12 Sungold tomatoes, halved
1 tablespoon fresh parsley leaves, chopped
½ cup fresh basil leaves
½ cup olive oil
¼ teaspoon fresh lime juice
4 tablespoons clarified butter
8 diver sea scallops
8 slices prosciutto di Parma
Chiffonade of squash blossoms

For the zucchini and corn: Remove the ends of the zucchini and cut the zucchini into quarters lengthwise. Remove the seeds by slicing away the center portion of each quarter. Cut on a bias into diamond shapes. Heat a sauté pan over medium-high heat. Add the grape seed oil and zucchini and season with salt and pepper. Cook, adding no color, until almost tender, about 2 minutes Remove the husk and silk from the corn, then remove the kernels from the cobs.

In a small pan, combine the zucchini, corn, 2 tablespoons of the stock, and ½ tablespoon of the unsalted butter. Simmer until the stock is reduced and the zucchini and corn are glazed. Add the tomatoes and parsley. Season with salt and pepper.

For the basil puree: Cook the basil in salted boiling water until it purees when rubbed between the thumb and first finger, about 8 minutes. Refresh in ice water. Drain the basil and place in a blender. Add the olive oil, season with salt, and blend until smooth.

Warm the remaining 4 tablespoons of the stock. Stir in about ¼ cup of the basil puree to create a thick sauce. Add the lime juice and season with salt.

For the scallops: Heat two sauté pans over high heat and add 2 tablespoons clarified butter to each pan. Season the scallops on both sides with salt and pepper. Divide the scallops between the hot pans and sear until golden. Turn the scallops, add the remaining 2 tablespoons unsalted butter, and baste until golden.

To plate: Divide the zucchini and corn among 8 warm plates. Fold a slice of prosciutto on each. Sauce the plates with the basil puree. Top with a scallop and garnish with squash blossoms.

ISLAY NEGRONI

In addition to the free-flowing Champagne, Auberge du Soleil deems it appropriate to offer a cocktail that reflects the colors of the sunset.

MAKES 1 COCKTAIL

1¼ ounces The Botanist Islay Dry Gin
1¼ ounces Campari
1¼ ounces Boissière Sweet Vermouth
Dash of orange bitters
Orange slice

In a tall glass filled with ice, stir together the gin, Campari, and vermouth. Strain the mixture with a fine sieve into a martini glass, or a highball glass filled with ice. Garnish with an orange slice.

PEACH PARFAITS

Parfait is French for "perfect," and such is Auberge du Soleil's peachy dessert. Ripe fresh peaches accented with verbena pastry cream create an elegant flavor combination.

MAKES 8 SERVINGS

Verbena Pastry Cream
1 quart whole milk
1 ounce verbena leaves, chopped
8 ounces sugar
2.8 ounces cornstarch
4 large eggs
2 ounces (½ stick) unsalted butter

Raspberry Conserve
14 ounces sugar
¾ ounce apple pectin
18 ounces raspberries

Ladyfinger Sponge Cake
6 large eggs, yolks and whites separated
7 ounces sugar
1 teaspoon pure vanilla extract
5½ ounces sifted cake flour

Champagne Syrup
1 cup Champagne
2 tablespoons simple syrup (one part sugar, one part water)

Verjus-Poached Peaches
¾ cup verjus
3 ounces sugar
4 medium peaches, cut into ¼-inch dice

Chantilly Cream
9 ounces heavy cream
1 teaspoon sugar
Pinch of kosher salt

For the pastry cream: In a saucepan, heat the milk to 190°F. Add the verbena leaves and steep for 5 minutes. Strain and return the milk to the pan.

In a bowl, combine the sugar, cornstarch, and eggs and whisk until light and airy. To temper the eggs, slowly whisk in one-third of the hot milk. Then slowly whisk the egg mixture into the milk in the pan. Simmer over medium heat for 2 minutes, until thick and elastic. Strain and stir in the butter until melted and combined. Cover with plastic wrap and place in the refrigerator to cool.

For the conserve: Whisk together the sugar and pectin in a bowl. Place the raspberries in a small pot and add the sugar mixture. Simmer for 20 minutes, until set. (Spoon a dollop onto a cold plate; the conserve is set when it slightly wrinkles when pushed.)

For the cake: Preheat the oven to 350°F. Line a rimmed baking sheet with parchment paper and spray the parchment with nonstick cooking spray.

In a stand mixer with the paddle attachment, combine the egg yolks and 4 ounces of the sugar and whisk on high until the volume triples. Add the vanilla and 1 teaspoon water. Fold in the cake flour until just combined. Set aside.

In a clean mixing bowl with clean beaters, make a French meringue with the egg whites and the remaining 3 ounces sugar: Beat the whites on high speed, adding the sugar a tablespoon at a time for 3 to 4 minutes, until medium peaks form.

Fold the meringue into the batter. Spread the batter evenly onto the lined baking sheet. Bake for 8 minutes, or until the cake bounces back when pressed. Chill the cake in the refrigerator for 2 hours.

With a 1-inch cutter, punch out 64 circles from the cake.

For the Champagne syrup: Combine the Champagne and simple syrup in a shallow bowl. Quickly submerge the cake circles in the syrup and gently press out the extra syrup. Reserve the cake circles.

For the poached peaches: Combine the verjus, ¾ cup water, and the sugar in a saucepan and bring to a boil. Add the diced peaches and immediately remove from the heat. Cool to room temperature, then chill.

For the Chantilly cream: Combine the cream, sugar, and salt and whip to soft peaks.

To serve: In each of 8 parfait glasses, place 1 spoonful of the conserve in the bottom, followed by 2 rounds of ladyfinger cake. Next, spoon on a layer of poached peaches, followed by a layer of pastry cream, then the Chantilly cream. Add 6 more rounds of ladyfinger cake, followed by layers of peaches, pastry cream, and Chantilly cream. Garnish with sliced peaches and a raspberry, if you like.

TIPS ON PAIRING FOOD WITH SPARKLING WINE

When serving a variety of sparkling wines to guests, "start light and move to richer wines," suggests Auberge du Soleil wine director Kris Margerum, and "aim for a nice steady pour down the center of the flute." (To invoke the wonder of Napa Valley, he recommends the local Schramsberg Blanc de Noir, which has a crisp flavor and a "faint persimmon color.")

Most sparkling wines boast minerality, adding a depth to savory, gamy flavors while also possessing a high acidity that cuts right through rich dishes. For his part, chef Robert Curry shows off these attributes by pairing sparkling wine with food that is either salty, including "fried things and crisp things," or food that is fermented or cured, for example, dishes that incorporate bacon, olives, or soy. "Those flavors tend to bring out the best in sparkling wines, making the perfect match."

WEEKAPAUG INN

WESTERLY, RHODE ISLAND

New England CLAMBAKE

AN ALL-AMERICAN SEASIDE FEAST THRILLS GUESTS WITH NATIVE LITTLENECKS, MUSSELS, AND LOBSTER COOKED TO PERFECTION ON A BED OF SEAWEED—PLUS ALL THE TRADITIONAL TRIMMINGS TO MATCH.

---

*Garden Party and Block Island Paloma Cocktails** *Red Bliss Potatoes with Caramelized Onions**
*Steamed Lobsters** *Native Littlenecks and Mussels with Chorizo and Roasted Corn**
Corn on the Cob *Roasted Corn Salad with Black Quinoa*

* RECIPE PROVIDED

J ust picture it—as the late summer sun goes down, a lucky group of adventurers quietly paddles a fleet of kayaks over serene, dark waters in one of Rhode Island's majestic salt ponds, the Quonochontaug. They beach their boats on the far shore and climb through marsh grasses and pine trees, and up and over the dunes. Then they settle in on a secluded sandy beach to watch a grand full moon rise over the ocean while sipping champagne. "It's something that people will remember for a long time," says Mark Bullinger, in-house naturalist and guide at the Weekapaug Inn, on the pond's western edge. "The sense of place really sticks with you."

Ever since the Buffum family opened the inn in 1899, the Inn's goal has been to provide guests with every opportunity to revel in the breathtaking setting. After all, as President James Garfield had remarked some years earlier, "We may divide the whole struggle of the human race into two chapters, first, the fight to get leisure; and then the second fight of civilization—what shall we do with our leisure when we get it?" At the Weekapaug Inn, the serious pursuit of leisure means indulging in the fresh air, marveling at wildlife, and soaking in the lush landscape. "It wraps around you, you're in it, not above it," says Bullinger. "A great blue heron sails over the yard, or, in the evening, the egrets fly by, while out on the pond fish jump out of the water." All summer long, a celebration of the great wilds culminates every Thursday night in a traditional New England clambake, honoring the old ways in every detail.

The Inn's backyard vantage point is close to perfect, on the edge of a sprawling estuary surrounded by marshes, and with a barrier beach separating the property from a sprawling ocean beyond. In keeping with that tranquility, there are no TVs in the rooms (though they can be installed upon request), and instead guests are treated to sightings of bald eagles or the occasional glossy ibis. They spend their days on guided beach walks, studying the native vegetation and learning about the glacial history of the land. With a twenty-foot net, Bullinger helps visitors pull in a big catch from the pond, transferring jellyfish, shrimp, and

If ever there were an ideal spot to stage a Rhode Island clambake, then certainly Weekapaug Inn is it. Situated at the edge of the great freshwater pond, with the ocean just beyond it, the place is idyllic and then some, offering guests every opportunity to take advantage of the great watery outdoors, from kayaking and paddleboarding to canoeing or going on "safari" with the in-house naturalist. "Lucky guests might spy a bald eagle or a glossy ibis."

Utterly old school, the weekly seafood suppers at Weekapaug Inn are as traditional as the red-checkered tablecloths fluttering on the tabletops, and the charming, friendly atmosphere invites guests to make new acquaintances. Justin Bothur, the inn's restaurant manager and sommelier, chooses a subtly rich chardonnay by Freeman Vineyard and Winery in California to pair with the evening's range of summery seaside dishes.

crabs into a viewing tank. The boathouse is fully stocked with kayaks, paddleboards, canoes, rowboats, and sailboats, and Bullinger captains two tour boats. The old-fashioned Quonnie Queen, a nearly silent electric boat, glistens with polished brightwork and seats six passengers in high-backed wicker chairs. There's also a shallow-draft motorboat—Bullinger's "safari vessel"—for actively exploring the hidden corners of the marsh and the pond's uninhabited islands, each guest armed with a set of binoculars.

The ideal finale of any back-to-nature outing is a big clambake down by the shore. The Weekapaug Inn, known for its abundant spread, hosts up to two hundred guests during the summer months, serving up clam chowder, corn, and roasted potatoes and, most spectacularly, the local littlenecks and fresh-caught lobsters that everyone craves. (Of course, it all goes so well with the Inn's minty Garden Party cocktail.)

In days gone by, this classic New England meal was called, more specifically, a "Rhode Island clambake," or a "shore dinner." Popular throughout the nineteenth century, summertime crowds ranged the coastline from resort to restaurant in search of the genuine article, filling large pavilions and dining halls that catered to the hundreds. The institution spread to Massachusetts and beyond, but it was also rooted in a sense of history, and offered a connection to Native American culture, as the clambake represents a proto-Thanksgiving. Cotton Mather, an early settler, wrote that a poor man, "inviting his friends to a dish of clams, at the table gave Thanks to Heaven who 'had given them to suck the abundance of the seas, and the treasures hid in the sands.'" In the eighteenth century, reenacting a "feast of shells," as food historian Katherine Neustadt points out, celebrated the idea that Native Americans introduced hungry new arrivals to the local seafood.

There is plenty to be thankful for at the Weekapaug Inn's table. Red-and-white-checkered tablecloths brighten the backyard, where all afternoon a hot bed of coals has been burning in the antique stone fire pit. "It's what you expect in New England: great local corn and seafood, and everything that's fresh and tasty," says chef Jennifer Backman, whose inventive side dishes include a roasted corn salad with black quinoa, charred lime, sweet pepper, fennel, and mint. In the fire pit, under a blanket of seaweed, native littlenecks and mussels simmer away with a little chorizo, roasted corn, and ale, while lobsters steam on a grate, covered in burlap until they are revealed, gloriously red in a billowing cloud of steam.

The fire pit, original to the property, flickers with a bonfire every night and is a favorite Weekapaug Inn gathering spot, with rocking chairs parked nearby. Guests wander down after dinner with all the essentials for s'mores making. (Good old Hershey's chocolate melts the best, Backman insists.) It's one of the subtle ways in which the inn's traditional ways foster camaraderie. People simply come together, whether out on the water, tucking in at the family-style clambake, or, once the sun sets, watching the stars through the inn's massive telescope. "We take advantage of the dark skies and the big horizon," says Bullinger. "We have great views of Saturn all summer long, and when people see it for the first time, they just start laughing. It's outrageously clear, and no one expects to see something that looks so real."

HOW TO STEAM LOBSTERS THE WEEKAPAUG INN WAY

Though some might argue that a proper bake should be performed in a pot placed inside a pit dug in the sand, the Weekapaug Inn's weekly seafood supper is about as authentic as they come. After all, historians point out that Rhode Island is where early American colonists first learned to love shellfish.

In anticipation of the delicious meal, in the afternoon the staff builds a big fire in the existing antique stone fire pit, creating a hot bed of coals. Once the fire is raging hot, they fill a huge stainless-steel rondo that sits atop a grate over the fire halfway with water. When the water boils, they add a huge batch of seaweed, following in the ancient Native American tradition, as well as a scattering of sliced lemons to the pot, contributing to the flavor. The lobsters sit on top of the seaweed bed and are covered with burlap that's been soaked in water to prevent burning. "In good conditions, the lobsters will cook in about ten minutes," says chef Jennifer Backman, "though if it is chilly or windy, they can take upwards of twenty-five minutes."

The evening's highlight comes when cooks pull back the burlap in a cloud of billowing steam to reveal the wonderfully red lobsters. Guests choose their lobsters on the spot, and the mallet-wielding cook splits the tails down the center, cracking both claws as well as the knuckles for easier eating.

GARDEN PARTY

The Weekapaug Inn's refreshing New England alternative to the mojito features fresh cucumber and mint from their garden and organic vodka distilled in nearby Ashford, Connecticut.

MAKES 1 COCKTAIL

3 cucumber slices, plus more for garnish
4 fresh mint leaves, plus more for garnish
1 teaspoon simple syrup or superfine sugar
1½ ounces Rime organic vodka
Fever-Tree club soda

Muddle the cucumber and mint in a highball glass. Add the simple syrup and fill the glass with ice. Add the vodka, finish with club soda, and garnish with cucumber and mint.

BLOCK ISLAND PALOMA

The inn's enhanced version of the classic Mexican staple uses freshly squeezed grapefruit juice and a pinch of ground sumac for a citrus and pepper note, then balances the libation with a local honey from Middletown, Rhode Island.

MAKES 1 COCKTAIL

1½ ounces blanco tequila (try a blanco mezcal for a
*   smokier approach)*
Pinch of sea salt
Pinch of ground red sumac, plus more for garnish
Fresh pink grapefruit juice
1 ounce honey syrup (two parts honey, one part hot water)
Fresh chervil sprig or another leafy green

Fill a highball glass with ice. In a cocktail shaker, combine the tequila, sea salt, and sumac. Fill with grapefruit juice and finish with the honey syrup. Shake and pour into the glass, adding more ice if necessary. Garnish with another pinch of sumac and the chervil.

RED BLISS POTATOES WITH CARAMELIZED ONIONS

A twist on the traditional potatoes served at a New England clambake, Weekapaug's potatoes offer all the comfort one has come to expect when dining waterside on a feast of steamed bivalves, lobster, and corn.

MAKES 8 TO 10 SERVINGS

5 pounds small Red Bliss potatoes, well washed
5 garlic cloves
1 bunch thyme sprigs
Kosher salt
½ cup olive oil
1 tablespoon coarsely cracked black pepper
Caramelized Onions (below)
2 tablespoons minced fresh thyme leaves

Place the potatoes, garlic, and thyme sprigs in a large pot and cover with cold water. Season liberally with salt. Bring to a simmer over high heat, then reduce the heat to low to maintain just below a simmer. Cook until the potatoes are al dente, 8 to 10 minutes, depending on the size of the potatoes. (Check doneness by inserting a wooden skewer into a potato; when there is just slight resistance and then the skewer slides through smoothly, the potatoes are done.) Cool the potatoes in the cooking liquid.

Heat a large skillet over medium-high heat and add the olive oil. Drain the potatoes and cut into quarters. When the oil just starts to smoke, carefully add the potatoes and cook, tossing occasionally, until caramelized, 4 to 5 minutes. Season with salt and the pepper. Add the caramelized onions and mix evenly until all the ingredients are intermingled and hot. Add the minced thyme, taste, and re-season if needed. Serve immediately.

Caramelized Onions

Salting the onions as soon as they hit the pan will extract excess moisture and help to evenly caramelize the onions.

MAKES 2 CUPS

¼ cup vegetable oil
4 medium Spanish onions, julienned (about 8 cups)
2 teaspoons kosher salt

Heat the vegetable oil in a very large skillet over high heat. Add the onions and immediately season with the salt. Cook, stirring periodically with a heatproof rubber spatula, until the onions start to take on color. Lower the heat and cook low and slow for 45 minutes, stirring throughout, until evenly caramelized.

NATIVE LITTLENECKS AND MUSSELS WITH CHORIZO AND ROASTED CORN

Steamed littleneck clams are the quintessential Rhode Island summer staple. Weekapaug Inn pairs the sweet, delicately briny flavor of native clams and mussels with spicy Portuguese sausage and local sweet corn. Allagash, a beer produced in Maine, rounds out the flavors and creates balance and harmony.

MAKES 8 TO 10 SERVINGS

6 ears of fresh corn on the cob, unhusked
¼ cup olive oil
1 pound chorizo, casings removed, crumbled
1 cup diced Spanish onions
Kosher salt
¼ cup thinly sliced garlic
5 pounds native littleneck clams, washed
1 (12-ounce) bottle Allagash beer
3 pounds Blue Hill Bay mussels, washed, beards removed
¾ to 1 cup (1½ to 2 sticks) Vermont unsalted butter
4 scallions, thinly sliced on the diagonal
Minced fresh parsley

Preheat the oven to 350°F.

Lay the unhusked corn on a baking sheet and roast for 25 to 30 minutes, until the husks are golden brown and the corn gives a little when squeezed. (You can also roast the corn in a convection oven at medium level fan for about 20 minutes.) Let cool. Remove and discard the husks and all of the silk. Run your knife down each side of the corncobs to remove the kernels. (Save the cobs for other applications; they make a great corn stock.) Set the corn kernels aside.

Heat the olive oil in a large rondo or large braising pan over medium-high heat. Add the chorizo, reduce the heat to medium, and allow the chorizo to render out some of the fat. Reduce the heat, add the onions, season with salt, and cook until translucent. Add the garlic and cook until soft and the aroma is extracted from the garlic. Add the clams and beer. Cover, return the heat to high, and cook for 9 to 11 minutes, until the clams just start to open.

Add the corn, mussels, and butter. Cover and cook for an additional 2 to 3 minutes, until all the shellfish are fully opened and the butter is melted. (If any shellfish do not open, discard them.) Season lightly with salt and finish with the scallions and parsley. Serve immediately.

Beach Taco FIESTA

AN ELEGANT BEACHFRONT FIESTA PROMISES WAVE AFTER WAVE OF
AUTHENTIC MEXICAN FLAVOR, WITH ALL THE REGION'S FAVORITE DISHES
LAID OUT IN AN UTTERLY BREATHTAKING SETTING.

Ginger Margarita   *Cast-Iron Octopus Carnitas Tacos*   *Braised Short Rib Tacos*
*Esperanza Guacamole, Ranchera Sauce, Tomatillo Salsa, and Spicy Tormenta Sauce**

*RECIPE PROVIDED

Azure waves roll into a secluded cove nestled between two steep, jagged bluffs at Esperanza, in Cabo San Lucas, far out on the tip of the Baja California Sur peninsula. It's the kind of place that invites romance, inspires deep thoughts, and sparks creative reveries. But while the sublime setting is pure drama, dining on the pristine private beach is utterly serene. And, in fact, when the table is laid with a delectable abundance of modern Mexican fare, the combination is nothing short of paradise.

Bounded by the Pacific Ocean on one side and the swirling tropical currents of the Sea of Cortez on the other, Baja serves up some of the freshest seafood around. Esperanza's chef Gonzalo Cerda works with three local fishermen, all of whom use nets instead of poles to ensure that his fish arrives each day in perfect condition. "When I say fresh, I'm not joking," he says. "They call at five or six in the morning to tell us what they've caught." For the property's ceviche bar, Cerda chooses sea bass, amberjack, mackerel, and bay scallop. For Cerda, who is Argentinian, and who trained in South America's top kitchens, creating a menu that maximizes Baja's unique flavors is a thrill. "As a chef, you can get bored," he explains. "You see everything the world has to bring you, but when I was visiting La Paz a fisherman showed me a clam as big as your hand with a deep brown shell, like the color of chocolate. He asked me if I wanted to taste it, then squeezed lemon on the live clam, right there. It was incredible, like when you eat a perfect oyster—that taste of the sea that just fills your mouth, salty and fresh." Naturally, local chocolate clams now boast a starring role on Cerda's menu, served grilled, steamed, citrus cured as ceviche, or in a chowder made with roasted poblano peppers.

In the resort's dining room, perched on the cliffs above Punta Ballena, each week the chef puts on an asado, a classic Argentinian barbecue featuring recipes from his childhood, but he also creates the perfect beachside meal highlighting the regional foods of Mexico. And as every aficionado knows, it wouldn't be a true Mexican fiesta without a well-crafted taco,

With each detail Esperanza celebrates seaside serenity, whether staging a chic taco dinner right on the sand—complete with a donkey bedecked in flower garlands—or by creating perfectly comfortable outdoor seating areas that offer dappled shade, while taking advantage of ocean breezes and breathtaking views. An appreciation for Cabo's legendary beauty extends to the menu, offering modernized classics from the Mexican canon, such as the Cabo Green margarita, served in a glass rimmed with chile piquin—a popular spice blend of salt, chile, and powdered lime.

which some food historians suggest originated in the eighteenth-century silver mines, where the word "taco" also referred to the small wrapped charges they used to excavate ore in the rock face. "The taco is the national dish of Mexico," says Cerda. "In each region it has its own flavor." Yet, Cerda's tacos are a cut above the typical batter-fried fish fare Baja made famous. Instead, he fills his tacos with braised short ribs rubbed with chili, or succulent octopus slow-cooked with bay leaf, rosemary, chilies, and thyme à la confit. (For this, the chef cooks the octopus in a three-legged cast-iron kettle given to him by his grandmother, one that has traveled with him for sixteen years.)

Still, as Cerda points out, "if the tortilla isn't good, the taco isn't good." At Esperanza, the kitchen staff grind their own white and blue corn to make masa, which the tortilla cook then hand presses and browns on a traditional comal grill over charcoal. "It gives the tortillas just a hint of smoky flavor," says Cerda.

Alongside rich guacamole made in a traditional volcanic stone bowl, green tomatillo salsa, and peppery ranchero sauce, Cerda serves tacos with his spicy tormenta sauce, brightening a tomato base with habanero, serrano, jalapeño, and chipotle peppers, as well as lemon, orange, and grapefruit juices, avocado, and a touch of Parmesan cheese.

Offering the perfect complement, the bar is fully stocked with a variety of Esperanza's signature cocktails, all boasting one-hundred-percent blue agave tequila, and including the Ginger Margarita, spiked with fresh ginger and fresh lime juice, and sweetened with agave nectar.

Though he once trained under some very demanding chefs, and though Cerda has years of experience as a professional, he learned how to make traditional Mexican cuisine the hard way—through his in-laws. "My wife is Mexican, and her mother and grandmother are amazing cooks," he says. But they're also very traditional. "When I first tried to come into the kitchen when they were cooking, just to see what they were doing, they said 'No-no-no-no-no!'" It took the persistent chef two months to gain access: "Just to watch. No questions. No speaking. No nothing," he recalls. Once he'd picked up all their tricks, he invited the whole family for an elaborate meal, serving his wife's mother and grandmother all the dishes he had learned through observing them. "I really did an incredible meal—and they loved it," he remembers, laughing. "But they're also very tough. They said, 'Now we are going to teach you. You know nothing.'"

At Esperanza the meal is served in traditional Mexican clay pottery, or *ollas de barro*, hand-painted, glazed earthenware cooking pots that, according to traditionalists, impart an incomparable flavor to each dish. Creating an outdoor bar on wheels using a handsome wooden cart— a *carreta de madera* like the one shown here, fabricated in Tlaquepaque, Jalisco—offers great versatility in outdoor entertaining. Stacked wooden crates, here and on the following page, provide shelving for the bartender, and create a sense of enclosure in the space.

GINGER MARGARITA

Esperanza's head bartender created this unique and refreshing cocktail a couple of years ago, inspired by the resort's philosophy of using fresh local, seasonal vegetables, fruits, and plants. Drink to good health.

MAKES 1 COCKTAIL

2 ounces silver tequila
1 ounce fresh lime juice
1 ounce agave nectar
3 fresh ginger slices
Lime wheel

Mix the tequila, lime juice, agave nectar, and ginger with ice in a cocktail shaker and shake for 20 seconds. Strain into a margarita glass, add ice, and garnish with the lime wheel.

CAST-IRON OCTOPUS CARNITAS TACOS

Chef Gonzalo Cerda of Esperanza knows that carnitas in Mexico don't have to be made with pork. Cooking the octopus in a very old cast-iron pot over mesquite wood coals contributes a special, lovely, smoky flavor to this unique delicacy.

MAKES 10 TO 12 TACOS

1 onion, cut in half
1 carrot, chopped
2 celery ribs, chopped
1/2 leek, chopped
8 bay leaves
Kosher salt
1 tablespoon whole black peppercorns
1 (1-pound) octopus
1 gallon canola oil
1 head garlic, cut in half
2 fresh rosemary sprigs
1/2 lime
1/2 orange
1 dried guajillo chile, cut in half
10 to 12 tortillas, warmed
Your choice of condiments and sauces (below and right),
  plus sliced onions, chopped fresh cilantro leaves, sliced
  cucumber, charred chiles, and lime wedges

Bring 2 gallons water to a boil in a large pot. Add the onion, carrot, celery, leek, 4 of the bay leaves, salt, and peppercorns. Add the octopus and boil for 15 minutes. Remove the octopus from the pot and dry with a paper towel. Set aside.

Heat the canola oil in a cast-iron pot over low heat. Add the garlic, rosemary, lime, orange, chile, and the remaining 4 bay leaves. When the oil is trembling on the surface, immediately add the octopus and cook for about 10 minutes. Remove and check to make sure it is tender, then cut it into small pieces.

To make your perfect taco: Place your favorite condiment in a warm tortilla and add the octopus carnitas followed by your choice of sauce.

Esperanza Guacamole
Authentic Mexican guacamole is a tradition, a technique, and a special selection of just a few ingredients that have to be perfectly combined to make it right. In short, guacamole is not as simple as everyone thinks. If you have the chance, pound the ingredients in a molcajete, the Mexican version of a mortar and a pestle; you will taste the difference.

Mash the flesh from 3 ripe avocados with a fork until smooth. Add the juice of 1 lime, 2 tablespoons chopped fresh cilantro leaves, 1 plum tomato (seeded and cubed), 1 tablespoon chopped onion, 1 serrano or jalapeño chile (seeded and minced), and kosher salt and freshly ground black pepper to taste. *Makes 4 servings*

Ranchera Sauce
To some, the B word ("burn") in the kitchen is completely prohibited. But there are some recipes where the final, tasty results depend on burning the ingredients. Like Esperanza's ranchera, a combination of vegetables that have been completely burned on a grill.

Prepare a grill with hot coals and grill the following whole vegetables until almost burned: 3 plum tomatoes, 1 small onion, 1/2 carrot, 1/2 celery rib, 1 jalapeño chile, 2 garlic cloves. Transfer to a blender and add 2 tablespoons fresh cilantro leaves and process to a chunky texture. Let cool, then add 3 tablespoons canola oil and kosher salt and freshly ground black pepper to taste. Mix well. *Makes 4 cups*

Tomatillo Salsa
The tomatillo, a staple of Mexican cuisine, contributes a pretty green color and perfect acidity to the traditional salsa.

Prepare a grill with hot coals and grill the following whole vegetables until almost burned: 12 green tomatillos, 1/2 onion, 1 1/2 jalapeño chiles, 2 garlic cloves. Let cool, then transfer to a blender. Blend well, then add the flesh from 1 ripe avocado, 3 tablespoons chopped fresh cilantro leaves, and kosher salt and freshly ground black pepper to taste. Mix to combine. Refrigerate immediately. *Makes 4 cups*

Spicy Tormenta Sauce
The name of this sauce says it all: It's a "storm" in your mouth.

Prepare a grill with hot coals and grill the following whole vegetables until almost burned: 3 habanero chiles, 2 serrano chiles, 1 jalapeño chile, 1/2 celery rib, 1/2 carrot, 4 garlic cloves. Combine 1/4 cup fresh orange juice, 1/4 cup fresh grapefruit juice, 1 tablespoon fresh lemon juice, 1 cup canned peeled tomatoes, and 1/4 cup minced chipotle chile in adobo in a small saucepan and cook over low heat until creamy, about 25 minutes. Transfer to a blender, add all the grilled vegetables, and process until chunky. Remove from the blender and let cool. Return to the blender and add 1/4 cup grated Parmesan cheese, 1/4 cup olive oil, and the flesh from 1/2 avocado and process again, until chunky. Season with kosher salt and freshly ground black pepper. *Makes 2 cups*

Esperanza employed several clever seaside lighting solutions using these clear bottle-shaped hanging lanterns to shield candles from the wind, while also opting for simple globe string lights hung in an easy crisscrossing pattern over the dining area.

GLENMERE MANSION

CHESTER, NEW YORK

Great Gatsby DINNER PARTY

AT GLENMERE, THE OPULENCE AND GRANDEUR ASSOCIATED WITH THE ROMANTIC ERA OF THE GREAT GATSBY COME TO LIFE WITH A GLAMOROUS THEME PARTY HARKENING BACK TO AN ADVENTUROUS, DECADENT PAST.

The Glenmere Gatsby   Selection of Canapés, including Tuna Tartare in Cucumber*, Deviled Eggs, Oysters, Olives, and Celery Sticks   Lobster Américaine*   Broiled Salmon with Sauce Mousseline and Tarragon Carrots*   Breast of Chicken Regency   Medallions of Venison with Sauce Poivrade and Chestnut Potatoes*   Baked Ham with Cognac   Gilded Age Dessert Selection*

*RECIPE PROVIDED

P lacid, imposing, and utterly glamorous, Glenmere Mansion is just the sort of place where F. Scott Fitzgerald and his famously fashionable wife, Zelda, would have liked to bunk down for a few days, their only worry which fountain to cavort in—the antique French fountain at the mansion's entrance, or the sculpted ironwork fountain in the garden's parterre? A fine-boned Italianate villa in New York's lower Hudson Valley, built in 1911 as a country retreat for industrialist Robert Goelet, the site is also, naturally, an ideal setting for a deluxe dinner in homage to "The Fitz," as the notorious Jazz Age couple was known in their heyday, and to F. Scott's masterwork, *The Great Gatsby*.

Glenmere is "a colossal affair by any standard," as Fitzgerald famously wrote of Jay Gatsby's place, complete with sweeping marble staircases and columned loggias and porticoes, all designed by Carrère and Hastings, the architects responsible for the New York Pubic Library. Its every detail harkens to that adventurous, decadent era when the Fitzgeralds railed against "dullness, sameness, predictability," as F. Scott wrote, riding in laundry carts at the Ritz, dancing on tabletops at the Waldorf, and being escorted out of the Biltmore after sliding down the banister, dizzying themselves in the revolving door, and performing handstands in the lobby. The Fitzgeralds flitted among friends' estates in the countryside beyond New York City, and the hijinks were all but continuous, with the couple going "on a party," as was the saying, as if they were going on a trip.

Honoring Gatsby with a themed dinner for twelve, and with a nod to the days when everyone from Babe Ruth to the Duke and Duchess of Windsor came to party at Glenmere, the inn's current owners, Dan DeSimone and Alan Stenberg, filled the mansion's motor court with shining vintage automobiles for guests to admire, including a mint-condition Rolls-Royce.

The deep-pocketed Goelets whiled away plenty of colorfully carefree hours at Glenmere until the 1940s. The place was sold, turned into a banqueting hall, and lost its luster. But in 2005, DeSimone and Stenberg spotted the crumbling hilltop property while driving past one day. "We were two guys, semi-retired and really bored," Stenberg remembers. Since 2007, maintaining and running the eighteen-room inn in the manner of a "rich uncle's estate" has consumed

In Glenmere's mahogany-paneled library, guests sampled one-bite canapés artfully arranged around and among the owners' wondrous collection of antiques and precious bibelots. Chef Gunnar Thompson set out not only deviled eggs and oysters, but, taking the Great Gatsby theme to heart, also simple dishes of olives and celery sticks—the "go-to hors d'ouevre of the day," he says.

the partners. (These days, guests are known to arrive by helicopter, with the inn's website providing the exact coordinates, while noting that the management appreciates prior notice of any landings.) They've restored Glenmere in a manner befitting its provenance, reviving the formal gardens created by landscape designer Beatrix Jones Farrand and naming the serene gray Duchess Suite after Goelet's sister, the Duchess of Roxburghe, who visited in the 1920s.

While Jay Gatsby's library was lined with carved English oak, party guests at Glenmere mingle in the mansion's sumptuous mahogany-paneled library, sampling the canapés and the evening's specialty cocktails, including the Glenmere Gatsby martini, blending Tito's vodka with passion fruit juice, lime juice, and cardamom and star anise syrup in a glass rimmed with crushed pink peppercorn. (To be sure, it's far superior to Scott's homebrewed bathtub gin made from juniper berry oil, coriander oil, aniseed oil, and sweetened with liquid rock candy syrup.)

Dinner guests passing into Glenmere's private China Room immediately discern Stenberg and DeSimone's passion for fine and rare china, which the duo has been collecting for twenty-three years. Even before they owned the mansion, they'd bid at auction on the sprawling sets that no one else wanted. "Who needs twenty-four of anything?" Stenberg laughs. Every treasure they've amassed is on offer to visiting hosts and hostesses—oyster plates, sterling salt-and-pepper shakers, and, of course, the thirty-five glorious sets of china. Stenberg says. "If it breaks, it breaks. It's all meant to be used," Stenberg says. The night of the dinner party the deep mahogany table was resplendent, blooming with white orchids and glittering with riches, including Stenberg's grandmother's inlaid sterling silverware and a towering pair of Italian candelabras.

Like the mansion's owners, executive chef Gunnar Thompson is something of a collector, scouring estate sales for antique cookbooks. In creating the evening's decidedly "old-school menu," he dusted off the classics and consulted historical menus from the fabled Delmonico's, a favorite New York haunt in days gone by. The meal opened with lobster Américaine, then came broiled salmon in sauce mousseline, "a really rich hollandaise with whipped cream folded in," says Thompson. "The taste is incredible, but I use it in sparing amounts!" Next came Breast of Chicken Regency. And then a medallion of venison with a poivrade sauce and chestnut potatoes. Finally, in a silver chafing dish, servers brought in a baked ham glazed with cognac and cherries. "People eat faster now, and I usually take that into consideration with a multi-course menu. But in those days, there was no rush—the meal itself was an event. I wanted to give guests that experience," the chef says. "In fact, one woman got up in the middle of the meal and sang opera, which seemed exactly like something that would have happened in those days." Naturally, dinner was just the prelude to a long evening to come. Gatsby would have been pleased, and the Fitzgeralds would have stayed 'til dawn—or longer.

In 1925, a women's magazine asked Zelda Fitzgerald for her favorite breakfast recipe. "See if there is any bacon, and if there is, ask the cook which pan to fry it in," she replied. "It is better not to attempt toast, as it burns very easily." Unlike a stay "chez Fitz," at Glenmere the morning after is just as glorious.

THE GLENMERE GATSBY

Glenmere Mansion salutes the cocktails of the Roaring Twenties with their singular Gatsby martini.

MAKES 1 COCKTAIL

Crushed pink peppercorns
2 ounces Tito's Handmade Vodka
1 ounce passion fruit puree
¾ ounce fresh lime juice
¾ ounce cardamom–star anise syrup (see Note)

Rim a martini glass with crushed pink peppercorns. Combine the vodka, passion fruit puree, lime juice, and syrup in a cocktail shaker. Shake and strain into the glass.

Note: To make cardamom–star anise simple syrup: Bring 1 cup sugar and 1 cup water to a boil. Pour over 1 whole star anise and 3 green cardamom pods in a heatproof bowl. Cool to room temperature and strain.

TUNA TARTARE IN CUCUMBER

Executive chef Gunnar Thompson says that the tuna is best taken from the apex of the triangular-shaped tuna loin as this has less sinew and is the most tender cut. Glenmere Mansion chooses sustainably caught yellowfin tuna fished off of Long Island, New York.

MAKES 6 TO 8 SERVINGS

1 English cucumber
2 tablespoons soy sauce
Grated zest of 1 lime
1 teaspoon ginger, peeled and grated
1 teaspoon sesame oil
1 teaspoon Sriracha chili sauce
½ teaspoon black sesame seeds
½ teaspoon white sesame seeds
4 ounces very fresh yellowfin tuna, chilled and finely minced

Slice the cucumber into ¾-inch-thick rounds. Scoop out the center of each with a melon baller to make a cup shape. Chill.

Whisk together the soy sauce, lime zest, ginger, sesame oil, chili sauce, black sesame seeds, and white sesame seeds. Just before serving, combine the tuna with the sauce. Spoon into the cucumber "cups" and serve immediately.

Glenmere's chef Gunnar Thompson dusted off select editions from his collection of cookbooks to replicate—and update—the most elegant dishes of the era, including a resplendent baked ham glazed with cognac and maraschino cherries. "With this menu, each course had it's own moment," says the chef, "and the guests took their time."

LOBSTER AMÉRICAINE

This classic lobster preparation has an unsubstantiated past but we do know it is delicious: A concentrated lobster sauce enriched with brandy and cream is served with freshly cooked lobster meat.

MAKES 8 SERVINGS

4 (1½-pound) live Maine lobsters

To prep the lobsters, insert a heavy chef's knife into the center of the belly of the lobster and push downward to split the head. Remove the claws and tail by twisting the body while holding the tail and claws respectively. You can use two of the heads from the lobsters to make the sauce.

Sauce Américaine

2 tablespoons vegetable oil
2 lobster heads, split and washed thoroughly, roughly chopped
2 tablespoons unsalted butter
2 cups mirepoix (finely diced mix of carrot, onion, and celery)
¼ cup tomato paste
2 tablespoons all-purpose flour
½ tablespoon paprika
1 cup brandy
1 cup vermouth
Cheesecloth sachet filled with 2 fresh thyme sprigs, 2 bay leaves, 12 whole black peppercorns
½ cup heavy cream
Kosher salt

For the Sauce Américaine: Heat a heavy saucepan over high heat. Add the vegetable oil and lobster heads and cook, stirring, until the heads have turned entirely red. Reduce the heat to medium. Add the butter, mirepoix, tomato paste, flour, and paprika and cook, stirring, for 5 minutes. Carefully add the brandy and vermouth. Bring to a boil, reduce the heat, and simmer until reduced by half, about 5 minutes. Add the sachet and 4 cups cold water. Simmer for 30 minutes. Strain through a fine sieve into a clean saucepan and add the cream. Reduce to a thick sauce consistency, about 10 minutes. Season with salt.

To cook the lobster: Bring a large pot of water (at least 2 gallons) to a boil. Season with salt; the water should taste of seawater. Place the claws in the pot and cook for 10 minutes. Add the tails and cook for 6 minutes.

Remove the lobsters to a cutting board. Split the tails with a heavy chef's knife and crack the claws with the back of a knife or shellfish cracker.

To serve: Reheat the sauce. Spoon some sauce into 8 individual serving bowls and top with the hot lobster pieces. Serve the remaining sauce in a gravy boat on the side.

BROILED SALMON WITH SAUCE MOUSSELINE AND TARRAGON CARROTS

Glenmere Mansion created this delicate dish with layers of rich and bright flavors to help invoke the Gilded Age of the 1920s. The Sauce Mousseline is actually a hollandaise sauce lightened with whipped cream. Chef Gunnar Thompson suggests over-seasoning the hollandaise because once you add the whipped cream, the sauce can become bland.

MAKES 8 SERVINGS

Tarragon Carrots

2 bunches baby carrots with tops
Kosher salt
3 tablespoons unsalted butter
Juice of 1/2 lemon
2 teaspoons chopped fresh tarragon

Sauce Mousseline

1/4 cup heavy cream
6 egg yolks
Juice of 1 lemon
1 teaspoon dry mustard
1 teaspoon Worcestershire sauce
2 dashes of Tabasco sauce
1/2 pound (2 sticks) unsalted butter, melted
Kosher salt

Salmon

1/4 cup (1/2 stick) unsalted butter, softened
8 (4-inch) salmon fillets

For the tarragon carrots: Scrub and peel the carrots. Cut off the tops, leaving just 1/2 inch. Place the carrots in a saucepan and cover with cold water. Season with salt and bring to a simmer. Cook, checking frequently, until just tender, about 7 minutes. Drain, reserving 3 tablespoons of the carrot cooking liquid.

Bring the cooking liquid to a boil in a large sauté pan. Add the butter, lemon juice, and tarragon. Add the carrots and cook, rolling them in the glaze, until well coated.

For the Sauce Mousseline: Whip the cream to soft peaks. Set aside.

Combine the egg yolks, lemon juice, mustard, Worcestershire sauce, and Tabasco in the top of a double boiler over simmering water. Whisk until the mixture becomes thick and warm to the touch. Remove the double boiler top and whisk in the melted butter, little by little, until the butter is incorporated and the sauce is emulsified. Season with salt.

Keep the sauce at room temperature and serve within 10 minutes of preparation. Just before serving, fold in the whipped cream. Serve in a saucier to pour over the salmon at the table.

For the salmon: Preheat the broiler to high. Smear the butter on a baking sheet.

Arrange the salmon fillets evenly on the sheet. Broil 6 to 8 inches from the heat, without turning, until well browned and the flesh is still light pink inside, 5 to 8 minutes, depending on the thickness of the fillets.

To plate: Arrange one salmon fillet and a few carrots on each of 8 dinner plates. Drizzle both salmon and carrots with the mousseline sauce at the table.

MEDALLIONS OF VENISON WITH SAUCE POIVRADE AND CHESTNUT POTATOES

Glenmere's chef Gunner Thompson likes to use the backstrap cut of venison, as it is the most tender piece of the deer. But the chef cautions that it is important to cook the venison no more than medium-rare, or this tender and lean cut will quickly become tough and strongly flavored.

MAKES 8 SERVINGS

Sauce Poivrade

3 tablespoons vegetable oil
1 pound venison trimmings and/or bones
½ onion, cut into large dice
½ carrot, cut into large dice
½ celery rib, cut into large dice
3 garlic cloves, crushed
3 cups dry red wine
1 cup port wine
2 juniper berries
1 bay leaf
12 whole black peppercorns, plus 2 tablespoons, crushed with a mallet
2 fresh thyme sprigs
2 quarts veal stock
2 tablespoons red wine vinegar (best quality available)

Chestnut Potatoes

2 pounds Yukon gold potatoes
10 whole fresh chestnuts
2 teaspoons vegetable oil
1 tablespoon unsalted butter
Kosher salt and freshly ground black pepper

Venison Medallions

3 tablespoons vegetable oil
3 pounds backstrap of venison, all sinew and fat removed
Kosher salt and freshly ground black pepper
3 tablespoons unsalted butter
2 fresh thyme sprigs
2 garlic cloves, crushed

For the Sauce Poivrade: Heat the vegetable oil in a large wide pot over high heat. Once it is shimmering, carefully add the venison trimmings and bones. Cook, turning occasionally, until well browned. Remove the meat and bones.

Add the onion, carrot, celery, and garlic to the pot and cook until browned. Return the meat and bones and add the red wine, port,

juniper berries, bay leaf, whole peppercorns, and thyme. Bring to a rolling boil, add the stock, and reduce to medium-low heat. Simmer, skimming frequently, until reduced and a sauce consistency, about 45 minutes.

Strain the sauce through a fine sieve into a clean pan; skim off any remaining fat. Add the crushed peppercorns and red wine vinegar. Gently reheat just before serving.

For the chestnut potatoes: Preheat the oven to 350°F.

Place the potatoes in the oven directly on the rack and roast for 60 to 80 minutes, until a knife slides into the center of the largest potato without resistance. Cool the potatoes until cool enough to handle and peel with a butter knife.

Cut the tips off the chestnuts, then cut an X on the flat side of each. Toss lightly in the vegetable oil and place on a heavy baking sheet. Roast for 20 minutes, or until the skin is peeling back from the nut and the nut is well browned. With a paring knife and a towel, carefully peel the chestnuts, removing the outer shell as well as the brown papery inner shell.

Just before serving, warm a skillet with the butter over medium heat. Add the potatoes and chestnuts and crush in the skillet with a fork. If necessary, place the skillet in the 350°F oven and cook just to warm the potatoes through. Once hot, remove and crush some more. Season with salt and pepper. Mold the potatoes and chestnuts into 4 rings.

For the venison: Heat a heavy skillet on high until very hot. Add the vegetable oil and swirl in the pan. Season the venison with salt and pepper. With tongs or a meat fork, add the venison to the pan and cook, turning, until well browned. Add the butter, thyme, and garlic. Turn the heat to low and cook, basting the meat with the butter, until an instant-read thermometer inserted into the center reads 110°F, or the meat starts to feel barely firm inside, about 12 minutes. Remove to a rack to rest for 5 minutes.

To plate: Slice the venison into 8 portions. Reheat the poivrade sauce. Place a potato-chestnut round on each of 8 plates and top with a venison medallion. Spoon the sauce over and around the potatoes and medallion.

Glenmere pastry chef Taiesha Martin consulted period cookbooks, researching what was served on ocean liners of the Gilded Age, including the *Titanic*. Her sculptural array included plump brown butter madeleines, lavender-clove Bundt cakes, passion-fruit-mousse bonbons, raspberry and lavender macarons, and chocolate-hazelnut eclairs.

Most evocative of all, however, were a dark chocolate espresso bombe, with layers of ice cream and devil's food cake, and baked Alaska, a domed sponge cake filled with vanilla ice cream hidden by toasted meringue. As one tastemaker wrote of the dish in 1879, when it was still a novelty, "Just before the dainty dish is served, it is popped into the oven, or is brought under the scorching influence of a red hot salamander. So you go on discussing the warm cream soufflé 'til you come, with somewhat painful suddenness, on the row of ice."

HOW TO CREATE A SENATIONAL THEMED PARTY

The success of a great theme party is when "guests feel lost and immersed in the party and are consumed by the wonderful details," says event designer Matthew Robbins, who created the Glenmere Gatsby fete. "Their senses will be awakened."

To begin, the theme chosen needs to suit the location, the season, and the guest list, he points out. However, in introducing a theme through the party's decor, don't go overboard. In creating the Gatsby party, the team's research provided the authentic details and accents, including cocktail napkins wrapped in a band of decorative paper, each printed by Regas Studio with a clever phrase of the Gatsby era—such as "You're the cat's meow."

Meanwhile, the tablescape was sophisticated, with eclectic touches that suggested the era. "A color palette or a perfect table setting can provide a loose framework," says Robbins. "Guests start to feel uncomfortable when things are too contrived." He ushered in a white, gold, and black palette, bringing plenty of candles to the tabletop as well as layered linens in velvets and embroideries, and clean, lush all-white floral arrangements held in black and gold antique vases. Yet, each place setting also offered a unique surprise, including that of the hostess, whose place card was held in a 1920s-era silver compact. "The small and thoughtful details are the things that guests remember," says Robbins. "They touch these pieces, interact with these objects and flavors."

let's dine

CANAPÉS
OLIVES AND CELERY

LOBSTER AMÉRICAINE

BROILED SALMON
CARROTS IN TARRAGON, MOUSSELINE SAUCE

BREAST OF CHICKEN REGENCY
ARROW LEAF SPINACH

MEDALLION OF VENISON
CHESTNUT POTATOES, SAUCE POIVRADE

BAKED HAM GLAZED WITH
COGNAC AND CHERRIES

WALDORF SALAD

PEAR AND VANILLA BEAN ICE

save room for...

ASSORTED CAKES

COFFEE AND CHOCOLATE BOMBE

PETIT FOURS

Natasha

HOMESTEAD INN-THOMAS HENKELMANN

GREENWICH, CONNECTICUT

CELEBRATION *of the Senses*

OFFERING GUESTS PURE INDULGENCE, THE HOMESTEAD INN–THOMAS HENKELMANN CREATED A PLEASURE-FILLED MEAL OF METICULOUSLY CRAFTED FRENCH HAUTE CUISINE TO BE SERVED IN THE INN'S LUSH GARDENS.

Champagne   Rum Daisy   Curry Velouté with Goujonnettes of Dover Sole**
Salmon in Brick with Osetra Caviar and Sauce Diable   Veal Tenderloin in Chanterelle Crust**
Apricot Trio   Brandy, Cognac, Scotch*

* RECIPE PROVIDED

In the grandest tradition, that of French haute cuisine, master chef Thomas Henkelmann delights the senses, creating meticulously enchanting meals at the Homestead Inn-Thomas Henkelmann in Greenwich, Connecticut. For nineteen years as the hotel and restaurant's chef and owner, alongside his wife, Theresa, he's soared in a world where carefully scrutinized meals receive star ratings and reputations are put on the line nightly. But in the intimate garden, as guests gather to experience Henkelmann's thrilling menu, all that simply seems to melt away. Surrounded by lush flowers and twinkling fairy lights, there's no doubt it will be a night to remember, full of delicacy, wit, and wondrous flavor.

Like Antonin Carême, the chef who founded French gastronomy at the beginning of the nineteenth century, Henkelmann apprenticed young, receiving a classical training among the three-star Michelin restaurants of Alsace, not far from his Black Forest home. Not surprisingly, Henkelmann's precise presentation is as immaculate as that of his illustrious predecessor, who cooked for King George IV, the Russian tsar, and Napoleon and Josephine, and who even invented the classical chef's toque. "When you begin young and work in certain restaurants in Europe, it's a very rigid process," says Henkelmann. "You learn to stay disciplined and focused."

With a wink at the past, Henkelmann flaunts his training with dishes such as a light curry velouté with goujonettes of Dover sole, served as a first course, each pristine plate encircled with jaunty harlequinesque diamonds of carrot, red pepper, and celery root. "I'm a contemporary chef, but one with a very classical background," says Henkelmann. "Thirty years ago I was lucky to learn from all the best European chefs who were pushing the boundaries."

In fact, dining à la Henkelmann is a master class in the heritage of French cuisine, and in its latest incarnations. Goujonettes are tiny fish that live in European lakes, but in the French kitchen serving any fish as goujonettes simply means cutting fillets into minnow-like strips. Meanwhile, Carême wrote of velvety velouté sauce in his masterwork, *The Art of French Cooking in the Nineteenth Century*, and his successor, Georges-Auguste Escoffier, considered France's next great chef, further honed the recipe while partnered with César Ritz and dishing up delicacies at London's Savoy and Carlton Hotel, and at the Ritz in Paris later in the nineteenth century.

Owner Theresa Henkelmann's Eurocentric flair and her love of eclectic layering create a whimsical ambiance in the former farmhouse. On the previous and following spread, the sparkling jewel-toned tablescape incorporates antique wine hocks and customized place cards designed by the master calligrapher Bernard Maisner as well as exuberant flower arrangements, each cleverly crafted in order to hide its container, to better blend into the garden.

As Escoffier explained, "Tastes are constantly being refined and cooking is refined to satisfy them." For Henkelmann, innovation and refinement mean serving a thick filet of Atlantic salmon, with a touch of Osetra caviar nestled into its tender core, and paired with a rendition of Escoffier's perfectly piquant sauce diable, rich with just a hint of spice, one that "tickles your throat," Henkelmann says. Honoring the Alsatian custom of baking en croute, out comes his tenderloin of veal in a chanterelle crust, the veal handsomely edged in a delicate layer of lacey chanterelles. Finally, an apricot trio makes for a delightful conclusion.

At the Homestead-Thomas Henkelmann, this potent combination—tradition matched by imagination—has proved irresistible, luring scores of devotees to the eighteen-room boutique hotel, built as a farmhouse in 1799, and its timber-framed restaurant, where there is rarely an empty seat. Recently, those throngs have included a *New York Times* reviewer who deemed the experience "extraordinary," penning a rare four-star homage, and noting that the occasion was "memorable in every category," thanks, in no small part, to the "creative food prepared and presented flawlessly."

However, as Voltaire pointed out, "Taste is not content with seeing, with knowing the beauty of a work; it has to feel it, to be touched by it." An extraordinary meal is an overall sensory experience, and that's where Theresa comes in. As an interior designer, her aesthetic perfectly matches that of her husband, layering and blending classical elements with a lighthearted touch. Guests at the inn are charmed by her eclectic touches—the mirror framed in gleaming porcupine quills, the winsome spider monkey sconces, or zebra club chairs. "For me walking into a room where it's all one thing, there's no soul," she says.

To heighten the mood in the garden that night, no detail was overlooked. Theresa engaged a calligrapher to create embossed and engraved name cards, each glistening with gold and a bejeweled elephant, trunk upraised, for luck. The florist was instructed to match the jewel tones of the tablescape, but also to hide the containers and vases amid blooms and branches, so that the whole might better blend into the garden. In honor of the evening, Theresa selected deliciously bright wine glasses she'd inherited from her grandmother. "Using those glasses is like scattering rubies, lapis, and amber onto the table," she says. "In creating the ambiance for our guests, we must always meet the level of the kitchen. You can't have mediocrity." While everything that the Henkelmanns do looks effortless, their approach is rigorous and methodical and creates an immensely luxurious atmosphere of hospitality. "The positive energy people feel upon arriving is so welcoming," says Thomas. "That's the first step in creating a wonderful experience." "When the curtain goes up, it's show time," Theresa agrees. "This is our guests' entertainment."

After several pleasure-filled hours drift by in the garden, bewitched guests, sated and content, retire to the veranda, and an evening that began with a glass of Krug champagne ends with rare brandy, cognac, or aged scotch and choice cigars. It's all part of the plan. "There needs to be a denouement. It's never dessert and good-bye," says Theresa. "That's not my style."

RUM DAISY

Astley Atkins, Homestead's bartender of seventeen years, created the Rum Daisy to celebrate the colors of summer.

MAKES 1 COCKTAIL

2 ounces light rum
Juice of 1/2 lemon
1 teaspoon grenadine syrup
1 teaspoon simple syrup (one part sugar, one part water)
Wedge or round of lemon

Fill a rocks glass with ice. Combine the rum, lemon juice, grenadine, and simple syrup in a cocktail shaker. Shake to combine and pour over the ice. Garnish with a wedge of lemon.

CURRY VELOUTÉ WITH GOUJONNETTES OF DOVER SOLE

Chef Thomas Henkelmann likes to offer a light hint of the exotic to set the stage for a sumptuous repast.

MAKES 6 TO 8 SERVINGS

Velouté
1/4 cup diced Spanish onion
1/4 cup sliced leek
1/4 cup diced fennel
2 tablespoons diced celery
1 garlic clove, minced
1/4 cup (1/2 stick) unsalted butter
1 teaspoon Madras curry powder
4 cups chicken stock
1 1/2 cups heavy cream
1/2 cup dry white wine
Dash of Pernod Ricard
Kosher salt and freshly ground white pepper

To Plate
1 (1-pound) side Dover sole, skinned, boned, filleted, and cut
   into 1-inch strips, then blanched
2 tablespoons red bell pepper cut into 1-inch diamonds
   and blanched
2 tablespoons celery root cut into 1-inch diamonds and blanched
2 tablespoons carrot cut into 1-inch diamonds and blanched
4 fresh basil leaves, cut into julienne

For the velouté: In a 3-quart casserole over low heat, sweat the onion, leek, fennel, celery, and garlic in the butter until soft without gaining color. Add the curry powder. Add the stock, cream, and white wine and bring to a boil. Reduce the heat and simmer for 20 minutes.

Puree the velouté in a high-powered mixer, then strain through a fine sieve. Add the Pernod and season with salt and pepper; depending on the taste, add more curry powder. Keep warm in a medium saucepan.

To plate: Place the sole strips and the diamond-cut bell pepper, celery root, and carrot in the centers of 6 or 8 soup bowls. Warm slightly in a low oven. Just before serving, add the basil and the warm velouté.

SALMON IN BRICK WITH OSETRA CAVIAR AND SAUCE DIABLE

Chef Thomas Henkelmann says that this modern play on the traditional Russian coulibiac "satisfies all my senses." The variation of textures is exciting.

Feuille de brick (also called brick pastry) is similar to phyllo dough but a bit thicker and with a different texture. You can buy it in specialty markets and online and is worth the effort to find it. You can use phyllo in a pinch, but it tears easily.

MAKES 6 SERVINGS

Salmon in Brick
6 (4-ounce) center-cut salmon fillets
3 ounces Osetra caviar
Juice of 1/2 lemon
Kosher salt and freshly ground black pepper
6 sheets feuille de brick
3 tablespoons extra virgin olive oil

Sauce Diable
1 shallot, minced
15 whole black peppercorns
1/4 cup Champagne vinegar
6 tablespoons brown veal stock
2 cups tomato juice
Kosher salt
Cayenne pepper

To Plate
12 baby bok choy leaves, blanched
1/2 cup sour cream
1 ounce salmon roe
3 ounces Osetra caviar

For the Salmon in Brick: Preheat the oven to 425°F.

Core the salmon fillets in the center and fill each with *1/2* ounce caviar. Season the fillets with lemon juice, salt, and pepper. Cut 6 sheets of *feuille de brick* the length of a salmon fillet and a little more than twice the width. Brush each with a bit of olive oil. Set a salmon piece on top of the *feuille de brick* and wrap tightly (with the ends exposed), making sure that the brick hugs the salmon fillet with no gaps. Seal each pastry with water or a bit of butter.

Heat a nonstick skillet over medium to medium-high heat. Add the remaining olive oil. Sear each side of the wrapped salmon until lightly golden, about 2 minutes. Place the wrapped salmon on a baking sheet and bake for about 2 minutes, or until the pastry is golden brown but the salmon is still rare (or medium-rare) on the inside. Let rest in a warm place for 3 to 5 minutes.

For the Sauce Diable: In a small pan, simmer the shallot and peppercorns in the vinegar until the vinegar is reduced by half. Add the stock and tomato juice and simmer for about 20 minutes. Strain the sauce and season with salt and cayenne. The sauce can be made and refrigerated 2 days ahead of time.

To plate: On each of 6 dinner plates, spread a circle of the diable sauce about 1 inch larger than the Salmon in Brick. Place 2 leaves of baby bok choy on the plates. Using a squeeze bottle filled with the sour cream, outline the sauce with the sour cream in a very thin line. Place a Salmon in Brick in the middle. Dot the rim of the plate with sour cream and alternate with some salmon roe. Finish with some of the caviar on top of the salmon.

VEAL TENDERLOIN IN CHANTERELLE CRUST

There is something captivating about the combination of chanterelles and veal: Homestead's transformation is created by the earthiness of the mushrooms and the delicacy of the meat.

MAKES 4 TO 5 SERVINGS

Chanterelle Sauce
2 tablespoons finely diced onion
2 tablespoons unsalted butter
1 pound fresh chanterelle mushrooms, cleaned
Juice of 1 lemon
Kosher salt and freshly ground white pepper
6 tablespoons heavy cream
Cheesecloth bouquet garni containing 1 fresh thyme sprig,
*   1 halved garlic glove, 1/2 bay leaf*

Chanterelle Mousse
5 ounces ground chicken breast
6 tablespoons heavy cream
Kosher salt and freshly ground black pepper
Cooked chanterelles (from sauce)

Veal Tenderloins
2 pieces caul fat
2 tips veal tenderloins (1½ pounds), each about 8 inches long

Tomato Fondue
1 shallot, finely diced
2 tablespoons extra virgin olive oil

2 large beefsteak tomatoes, peeled, cored, and finely diced
6 fresh basil leaves
Kosher salt and freshly ground black pepper

To Plate
Fingerling potato puree
Steamed or blanched baby vegetables

For the chanterelle sauce: Sweat the onion in the butter in a saucepan until translucent. Add the fresh chanterelles, along with the lemon juice and a little salt and white pepper. Cover the pan and cook for 5 minutes, until the chanterelles are cooked through. Remove the chanterelles and reduce the liquid left in the pan by half. Using paper towels, squeeze out some of the remaining mushroom juice and set the mushrooms aside.

Add the cream and the bouquet garni to the pan and reduce again by half. Adjust the seasoning of the sauce and strain through a fine sieve. Keep warm until ready to serve (within 30 minutes).

For the chanterelle mousse: In a food processor, mix the ground chicken and cream until smooth and shiny. Season with salt and black pepper and fold in the cooked chanterelles.

For the tenderloins: Spread out the 2 pieces of caul fat on a cutting board. Spread on a thin layer of the chanterelle mousse, 3 inches wide and 8 inches long. Top each with a tenderloin. Spread the remaining mousse on top of the tenderloins in a thin layer less than 1/2 inch thick. Wrap the tenderloins tightly with the caul fat, then tie with butcher's twine to help keep the shape. Refrigerate for 1 hour.

Preheat a convection oven or a standard oven to 400°F.

Place the tenderloins in a small nonstick pan and roast until medium-rare, 15 minutes in either oven. Set in a warm place to rest for 5 to 8 minutes.

Meanwhile, for the tomato fondue: Sweat the shallot in a saucepan with the olive oil until translucent. Add the tomatoes and basil and season lightly with salt and black pepper. Simmer slowly, watching and stirring, for 3 to 5 minutes, until the fondue has a slightly stewed consistency but is still moist.

To plate: Garnish warm serving plates with potato puree, tomato fondue, and a baby vegetable. Slice the tenderloins into medallions and set on the plates. Spoon some of the chanterelle sauce around it. Serve immediately.

APRICOT TRIO

Creating a trio of distinct but separate preparations from the same ingredient can be a challenge. But the different textures, combination of ingredients, and tastes speak to the art and creativity of nature. Feel free to use quality store-bought apricot sorbet and frangipane to cut down on the prep time.

MAKES 8 SERVINGS

APRICOT STRUDEL

Juice of 1 lemon
6 ounces sugar
8 apricot halves, unpeeled
8 ounces all-purpose flour
1 large egg yolk
2 tablespoons vegetable oil
Pinch of kosher salt
2 ounces (1/2 stick) unsalted butter, melted
5 ounces Frangipane (right, or store-bought)

For the strudel filling: Combine 2 cups water, the lemon juice, and sugar in a 2-quart saucepan and bring to a simmer. Add the apricots, return to a simmer, and remove the pan from the heat. The apricots should be cooked but still firm and holding their shape. Let cool, then refrigerate in the poaching liquid.

For the strudel dough: Combine the flour, egg yolk, vegetable oil, 1/2 cup water, and salt in a stand mixer with the dough attachment and mix for about 5 minutes, until smooth. Cover the bowl tightly with plastic wrap and let the dough rest at room temperature for 30 minutes. Preheat the oven to 375°F. Line a baking sheet with parchment paper.

To assemble the strudel: Roll out the strudel dough as thinly as possible. Spread a tea towel on the counter, lift up the dough, and use the backs of your hands to pull the dough as translucent as possible to a rectangle about 24 by 6 inches. Place on the towel and brush lightly with the melted butter.

Using a soupspoon, place 8 portions of frangipane, each a little less than 1/2 ounce, in a line about 1 1/2 inches from one long edge of the dough. Set an apricot half on top of each frangipane portion. Fold 1 1/2 inches of the long edge over the apricots. Then, using the towel as a guide, fold the dough and apricots over twice, forming a long rectangle about 1 1/2 by 24 inches. Cut out the 8 pieces of strudel and press together the edges to seal.

Place the strudel on the baking sheet and bake for about 10 minutes, until the dough is golden brown.

APRICOT SORBET

16 ounces apricot puree
6 ounces simple syrup (one part sugar, one part water)
Juice of 1 lemon
Apricot liqueur

Combine the apricot puree, simple syrup, lemon juice, and apricot liqueur and churn in an ice-cream maker, according to the manufacturer's instructions. Reserve in the freezer until needed.

APRICOT MARZIPAN TARTES

Marzipan

2½ ounces unsalted butter, softened
4 ounces sugar
1 large egg
1 ounce all-purpose flour
1 knife-tip baking powder
6 ounces almond paste
A splash of Grand Marnier

Apricot Mousse

5 ounces apricot puree
2 ounces sugar
3 gelatin sheets, soaked for about 30 seconds until soft
2 large egg whites
4 ounces heavy cream, whipped to soft peaks

Crust Dough

8 ounces (2 sticks) unsalted butter, softened
7 ounces sugar
3 large eggs
20 ounces all-purpose flour

Apricot halves, poached as for the strudel (left) and sliced

For the marzipan: In a large bowl, combine the butter and sugar and whisk until smooth. Slowly add the egg, flour, and baking powder, then the almond paste and Grand Marnier. Store the marzipan in the refrigerator until ready to use.

For the apricot mousse: In a small saucepan over low heat, warm the apricot puree with 1 ounce of the sugar. Transfer to a large bowl and stir in the soaked gelatin sheets. In a medium bowl, whisk the egg whites with the remaining 1 ounce sugar to soft peaks. Fold the whipped cream into the apricot mixture, followed by the egg whites. Refrigerate for a minimum of 3 hours.

For the crust dough: In a stand mixer with the paddle attachment, beat the butter with the sugar, then slowly add the eggs and then the flour. Knead until smooth. Refrigerate the dough for 1 hour.

Roll out the dough thinly and use it to line a 10 by 3-inch springform pan. Spread the marzipan about ½ inch thick on top. Bake for 5 minutes, until baked on the edges and still soft in the center. Let cool, then cut out eight 1½-inch rounds.

To assemble the tartes: Place a crust round into a ring mold that is 1½ inches wide and 2 inches high and top with apricot mousse. Repeat to make 8 tartes. Refrigerate for at least 3 hours. Top with sliced apricots before serving.

To Plate the Apricot Trio

Apricot coulis
Raspberry coulis
Yogurt coulis, sweetened with confectioners' sugar and lime juice added to taste
Strawberries

Using one plastic squeeze bottle per coulis, form circles with the apricot coulis, raspberry coulis, and yogurt coulis. Cross the coulis lines with a toothpick for decoration. Place a warm strudel, an apricot tarte, and a spoonful of sorbet on the coulis. Finish the plate with a strawberry dipped in apricot glaze.

Frangipane

3 ounces (¾ stick) unsalted butter, softened
3 ounces sugar
2 large egg yolks
Grated zest of ½ orange
Grated zest of ½ lemon
3 ounces almond flour
Pinch of kosher salt
2 large egg whites

In a medium bowl, mix the butter with 1½ ounces of the sugar until creamy. Slowly add the egg yolks, orange zest, lemon zest, almond flour, and salt. In a separate clean medium bowl, whisk the egg whites with the remaining 1½ ounces sugar and add it to the flour mixture.

Celebrating at the Homestead Inn-Thomas Henkelmann means a long, lingering finish, which might well include a Rum Daisy. "In Victorian times the men retired after the meal with port and the ladies with sherry," Theresa Henkelmann points out. "Now it's a more modern take, with brandy, cognac, aged scotch, or some wonderfully refined spirit." That also means cigars on the veranda. The inn's staff is highly trained, guiding guests in their selection from the Davidoff cigar service and offering a handful of choices displayed in the most handsome humidor.

MEADOWOOD NAPA VALLEY

ST. HELENA, CALIFORNIA

Wine Harvest DINNER

A LAVISH AUTUMNAL MEAL IN HARMONY BOTH WITH THE TERROIR AND THE SEASON BRINGS FRIENDS TOGETHER FOR A TASTE OF THE BEST NAPA VALLEY HAS TO OFFER.

---

*"The Ocean" Amuse Bouche** *Meadowood Garden Beet Salad** *Sweet Potato Gnocchi with Vadouvan Crema** *English Cucumber and Radish Salad** *Sea Bass with Potato Scales* *Duck Confit**

* RECIPE PROVIDED

A hint of the wild has hung in the air over Napa Valley since well before 1880, when Robert Louis Stevenson called the place "one of man's outposts in the wilderness." And at no other time of the year is a visitor's visceral connection to the land, to the terroir, as wildly evocative as it is at harvest time. An excited buzz seems to electrify the valley's thirty-mile stretch each autumn when the vines are heavy with fruit. "Literally, you can smell it—the whole valley smells like wine and grapes for a few weeks," says Patrick Davila, Meadowood's director of wine and cuisine and the hotel manager. In the midst of that heady atmosphere, Meadowood, an estate tucked into a forested hillside, hosts an exuberant Harvest Dinner like no other, with a menu showcasing the best of the season's bounty—from the Meadowood garden beet salad and sweet potato gnocchi to duck confit—as well as some of the most coveted local wines around.

Charles Krug opened Napa's first commercial winery in 1861, following pioneering vintner Hamilton Walker Crabb, who experimented with four hundred different kinds of grapes, hoping for a winner. The hearty farmers who followed battled phylloxera and just survived Prohibition—by producing only sacramental wines. Today, some four hundred vineyards fill the valley's 788 square miles with vines. The valley's rough-hewn history and its stunning natural beauty ignite a passion for the place, as does its wine.

When a young Stevenson arrived in 1880 for an unconventional honeymoon with his new bride, the local wine business was just taking off, and so was he. (*Treasure Island* and *The Strange Case of Dr. Jekyll and Mr. Hyde* were yet to come.) The happy couple camped out in the bunkhouse of a deserted mining camp at the base of Mount Saint Helena (now Robert Louis Stevenson State Park), dodging rattlesnakes and hauling water from the stream, escapades he later turned into the book *The Silverado Squatters*, but they also toured several newly minted vineyards. "In this wild spot, I did not feel the sacredness of ancient cultivation. It was still raw," Stevenson wrote of one visit. "Yet the stirring sunlight, and the growing vines, and the vats and bottles in the cavern made a pleasant music for the mind." Better yet, what he tasted in those rugged cellars was enough to convince Stevenson of the valley's future. "The smack of California earth shall linger on the palate of your grandson," he predicted. And so it does.

"During the harvest there's a sense of sheer excitement and anticipation of what this year will bring in years to come," says Davila. Trucks whiz past carting deep purple Cabernet Sauvignon grapes and the fresh green Chardonnay, the region's most widely planted varietals.

For decades Napa Valley has been an ultra-civilized outpost overlooking the sun-streaked wilderness, one that gives city dwellers a taste of the good life and a deep-rooted connection to the land. At harvest time, a scent of grapes hangs in the air and guests at Meadowood are perfectly poised among the valley's four hundred vineyards. "During the harvest every vintner in town offers the chance to taste some of the most recent releases," says director of wine and cuisine Patrick Davila, who oversees the property's daily wine tastings and private vineyard tours.

It's a busy time at Meadowood, where the restaurant's tables are filled with winemakers and visiting vintners all sampling each other's wares. "Everyone is in town during the harvest," Davila continues, "and it's a chance to taste some of the most recent releases, from three to four years ago." The estate holds wine receptions every day, but also conducts exclusive vineyard tours that offer behind-the-scenes access at vineyards not otherwise open to the public.

At Meadowood, the high point of the year's harvest is an intimate outdoor dinner in a chic dark-wood and leather entertaining structure created just for the occasion. Staged in the meadow, with awe-inspiring views of the grand expansive landscape, guests relaxed in leather club chairs and sipped wine around a fire pit. The dinner table, decorated with weathered manzanita branches, persimmons, foraged leaves, and a scattering of acorns, all gathered on the property, perfectly set the tone for chef Alejandro Ayala's menu celebrating the local terroir in every which way.

"We have our own culinary garden and everything is inspired by what's coming out of the ground that week," says Davila. At the harvest dinner, heirloom beets are sprinkled with "beet soil," made from the pulp of juiced beets, and served alongside round dollops of fresh chèvre. Dainty sweet potato gnocchi come in a light cream sauce spiced with vadouvan, a French curry blend. Duck confit is a rich succulent dish appropriate for the season. Sea bass fillets wrapped in a layer of potato scales are drizzled with a peppery red wine sauce. "The chef loves to showcase the flavor of a select few ingredients," says Davila. "That way the flavors speak for themselves, just as with a good wine."

Each dish is met by a fleet of fascinating California wines, including those from Harlan Estate and from Screaming Eagle. However, the pairings are anything but didactic. "We like to serve this kind of meal family style, and the wines are the same—some people trying this one, some trying that—offering more opportunities to explore and a lot more fun," Davila explains.

Davila himself enjoys the contrast of the tannins of Harlan Estate's The Maiden with the rich duck confit, but in wine country, when a single dish is paired with a single wine, he explains, the atmosphere can turn critical, and can lead to disappointment. "When you do a meal with strict pairings, you experience one person's opinion. Sometimes that can be interesting, but when twelve people express twelve opinions, there's a lot more to talk about. It's a conversation," he notes. "Having the opportunity to experience more than one flavor profile is something that can spark the senses, and rigidly classic pairings can leave out the chance for surprise or discovery." After all, discovery is what it's all about—that and romance.

There's plenty to discover without ever leaving the table. At nightfall, the lights glowing in the inn's windows, a cool breeze lifted and blew down the valley, and anyone could see just why generations of travelers have fallen in love with this place. "Indeed it would be hard to exaggerate the pleasure that we took in the approach of evening," Stevenson wrote of his Napa soujourn. "The shadows lengthened, the aromatic airs awoke, and an indescribable but happy change announced the coming of the night. . . . It was good to taste the air," Stevenson concluded, "good to mark the dawning of the stars, as they increased their glittering company."

Exuberant touches make the evening memorable, including the meandering autumnal centerpiece. Instead of cut flowers, pomegranates, persimmons, acorns, and manzanita branches foraged on the property create a colorful and naturalistic tapestry alongside an array of leaves, each individually clear-coated to keep them crisp and bright. Just as much care goes into a dish that chef Alejandro Ayala calls "The Ocean" (far right), made with Pacific oysters, Mendocino sea urchin, and Osetra caviar, with just a hint of crème fraîche and lemon zest. Rather than serve each tantalizing spoon on a bed of shaved ice, Ayala goes for drama, filling a metal bowl with dry ice, hidden by a mesh guard covered by smooth river rocks. Dousing the stones—and the dry ice below—with a bit of hot water just before setting the spoons in place invigorates rising wisps of cold haze.

MEADOWOOD GARDEN BEET SALAD

This beet salad is one of Meadowood's favorite dishes during the summer harvest season. The beets can be small heirloom varietals of all colors and stripes (literally). Chef Alejandro Ayala recommends taking some artistic license with the presentation; he cuts the beets into various shapes as well as paper-thin cross sections. The salad is at once both bright and earthy, and the pistachio "soil" is an unexpected, at-home, twist.

MAKES 12 SERVINGS

Roasted Beets

5 pounds assorted beets
3 tablespoons sugar
3 tablespoons kosher salt
1/4 cup extra virgin olive oil

Orange-Lemon Dressing

1/4 cup fresh orange juice
1/4 cup fresh lemon juice
1 cup extra virgin olive oil
Kosher salt

Pistachio-Beet "Soil"

6 large beets
1 cup pistachio nuts
Maldon sea salt
1/4 cup extra virgin olive oil

Whipped Goat Cheese

2 1/4 cups heavy cream
3 sheets gelatin, bloomed (soaked for 5 minutes in cold water)
10 to 12 ounces fresh goat cheese

To Plate

Maldon sea salt
Baby beets, shaved with a mandoline
Micro red amaranth or other greens
Black Hawaiian sea salt (optional)

For the beets: Preheat the oven to 300°F.

Remove the stems and wash the beets well. In a roasting pan, combine the beets, sugar, kosher salt, olive oil, and enough water to cover the beets halfway. Cover the pan with aluminum foil and roast the beets until fork tender, about 45 minutes, depending on the size of the beets. Let sit until cool enough to handle. Remove the peels by hand or using a kitchen towel. Cut the beets into an assortment of sizes and shapes (planks, cubes, small ones whole, or just cut in half or quarters).

For the dressing: Combine the orange juice, lemon juice, olive oil, and kosher salt in an airtight container. Shake until emulsified.

For the "soil": Preheat the oven to 250°F. Line a baking sheet with parchment paper.

Juice the beets in a juicer. Reserve the juice for another use. Measure out 2 cups of the beet pulp.

Spread the beet pulp evenly on the baking sheet. Place in the oven and dry, stirring and turning the tray intermittently, until completely dehydrated, about 40 minutes. Set aside to cool.

Raise the heat to 300°F. Toast the pistachios for 4 to 6 minutes, or toast in a sauté pan over medium-low heat. Let cool. Grind the pistachios well in a food processor.

In a medium bowl, mix the dehydrated beets and ground pistachios, seasoning with the sea salt and stirring in the olive oil. It should have a crumbly, coarse consistency.

For the goat cheese: Whip 2 cups of the cream to medium peaks. Set aside in the refrigerator.

In a small sauté pan, heat the remaining 1/4 cup cream to about 115°F, just warm enough to melt the bloomed gelatin. Add the gelatin to the cream and incorporate. Place the goat cheese in the bowl of a stand mixer fitted with the paddle attachment. Pour the cream and gelatin mixture over the cheese and mix until combined and the consistency of paste. Place the bowl in an ice bath and whisk to cool quickly. (Be sure to whisk continuously so the gelatin sets properly.) Once the mixture is cool, fold in the whipped cream in batches, gently folding to keep as much air as possible in the cream.

To plate: Lightly coat the roasted beets with dressing to taste and season with a touch of sea salt. Place a base layer of beets on serving plates. Sprinkle the soil in a few places. Continue building with layers of beets of different sizes, shapes, and colors. Lightly dress the shaved beets and arrange them throughout the cooked beets. Sprinkle with more soil. Add a quenelle or small dabs of whipped goat cheese and garnish with the amaranth. If you like, finish the top of the goat cheese with black Hawaiian sea salt for some extra contrast.

SWEET POTATO GNOCCHI WITH VADOUVAN CREMA

On a cool autumn day, there is something wonderfully warming about creating fresh, homemade pasta. Meadowood uses sweet potatoes to create pillow-y dumplings that sit atop a bed of whipped cream seasoned with vadouvan, a French curry powder. Traditionally a hearty meal, these particular dumplings can be served as an entrée or as a lighter accompaniment.

MAKES 12 SIDE SERVINGS OR 4 ENTRÉE SERVINGS

Sweet Potato Gnocchi

3 sweet potatoes or yams
2 large eggs
½ cup ricotta cheese
½ cup grated Parmesan cheese
1 cup all-purpose flour, plus more for rolling
Kosher salt and freshly ground black pepper
10 cups rice bran oil

Vadouvan Crema

1 cup heavy cream
½ cup crème fraîche
2 tablespoons vadouvan

To Plate

1 cup micro amaranth

For the gnocchi: Preheat the oven to 300°F.

Place the sweet potatoes on a baking sheet and roast until tender, 35 to 40 minutes. Remove from the oven and let cool. When cool enough to handle, remove the skins and pass the flesh through a tamis, food mill, or potato ricer.

In a large bowl, mix together the eggs, ricotta, Parmesan, and flour to make a dough. Add the sweet potatoes and mix until fully integrated. Season with salt and pepper.

On a wooden surface, create a thin layer of flour. Roll the dough into long strands ¾ inch thick, then cut into 1½-inch pieces. Use a gnocchi paddle or fork to imprint grooves. Place the finished gnocchi on a floured baking sheet and place in the freezer for at least 30 minutes. Once the gnocchi are frozen, they will keep for weeks.

To cook the gnocchi, heat the rice oil in a large saucepan to 350°F. Add the frozen gnocchi and fry until the dough rises and achieves a golden color, 3 to 5 minutes. (Depending on the size of your pan, you may need to fry the gnocchi in small batches to maintain the temperature of the oil.)

For the crema: In a medium bowl, whip the cream to soft peaks. Fold in the crème fraîche and vadouvan and continue to whip until fully incorporated.

To plate: Using a serving spoon, spread a ½-inch base of crema on a serving plate. Place the gnocchi on top and garnish with the micro amaranth.

ENGLISH CUCUMBER AND RADISH SALAD

Meadowood's garden twist on the Greek classic is prepared with only a handful of ingredients. Light and cool, the salad can be served during the warmer first days of autumn to refresh, or as a garnish for dishes with a bit more heat as the season spices up. It is also lovely with Ora King salmon.

MAKES 12 SERVINGS

1 cup Greek yogurt
2 tablespoons chopped fresh dill, plus sprigs for garnish
Juice of 3 lemons
Kosher salt and freshly ground black pepper
3 English cucumbers, peeled, halved lengthwise, seeded, and sliced
1 bunch baby radishes, thinly sliced on a mandoline, plus whole or sliced radishes for garnish

In a small bowl, mix together the yogurt, chopped dill, and lemon juice and season with salt and pepper. In a large bowl, combine the cucumbers and radishes with the yogurt dressing. Garnish with dill sprigs and additional radishes.

DUCK CONFIT

Duck confit done beautifully is something to behold. Meadowood chef Alejandro Ayala's recipe is simple and exquisite. He takes the time to remove the thigh bones from each duck leg, which can be done at home or by your local butcher shop. This one thoughtful step ensures that the end result will be fork tender and easy for guests to enjoy, and still beautifully presented.

MAKES 12 SERVINGS

12 duck legs, skin on
Kosher salt
3 pounds duck fat, melted
5 garlic cloves
1 tablespoon whole black peppercorns
3 bay leaves

Remove the thigh bone from each leg by making a single cut on each side. Once the leg bone is removed, open the leg meat and season the inside liberally with salt. Roll each section back together and tie with butcher's twine to hold the shape. Transfer the duck legs to a roasting pan. Cover first with plastic to create a tight seal, and again with aluminum foil. Refrigerate overnight or for at least 12 hours.

Preheat the oven to 300°F.

Remove the foil and plastic wrap. Add the duck fat, garlic, peppercorns, and bay leaves to the pan. Cover with a lid or aluminum foil; it should be a secure seal. Bake for 3 to 3½ hours, until the legs are tender and the meat can be separated with a fork but still hold its shape. Serve immediately or hold for later use. Finished confit will keep in the refrigerator for up to 1 week.

Remove the duck legs from the cooking liquid. Heat a nonstick sauté pan over medium-high heat. Add the duck legs and sear until the skin is crisp. (Duck skin is very delicate, so a nonstick pan is recommended.)

ENGOYING WINE

"Enjoying wine has a lot to do with the environment in which it's served, just as it does with how the grapes are grown," says Meadowood's director of wine and cuisine Patrick Davila. When selecting wines, a host should consider the weather, he points out: "No one wants to drink rosé when it's forty-five degrees." Additionally, it's the host's duty to ensure wines are served at the intended temperature. Red wine is usually served too warm, Davila says, and white wine too cold. "The flavors don't develop in the glass as they should."

It's important to learn about what you're serving, Davila suggests, and knowing a little about where the wine came from and its context. Yet beware of overenthusiasm. "Using the meal to demonstrate the abundance of your personal wine knowledge can really stop the evening from being fun," he says. "The more esoteric the wines, the less they'll be understood." His rule of thumb is keep it simple, serving three or four wines at most, including something fantastic and little known, but also something that your guests are familiar with "so that they have an ability to compare the wines," he explains.

After all, sharing a meal is what brings friends together. "Often people rely on a known brand in order to make their decisions in choosing a wine, but that doesn't always do it. You should serve something you are passionate about."

Courtyard Lights DINNER PARTY

AT HISTORIC PLANTERS INN, TWINKLING LIGHTS, MASSES OF CANDLES, AND GLITTERING GOLDEN DETAILS TRANSFORM A QUIET URBAN OASIS INTO A FANTASTICAL WONDERLAND FOR AN EVENING OF FINE DINING.

Planters Punch*   *Trio of Soups*   *Roasted Wreckfish with Leek-Crab Sauté**
Pan-Seared Scallops with Bibb Lettuce, Lobster, and Citrus Broth*
Tea 'Tini*   *Peninsula Grill's Ultimate Coconut Cake**

* RECIPE PROVIDED

idden at the end of an antiquated brick alleyway and through a wrought-iron gate lies Charleston's most picturesque dining spot, a courtyard lit with carriage lanterns and palmettos rustling overhead. Planters Inn, at the corner of Market Street and Meeting Street, provides a decadently soulful oasis in the very epicenter of the great city's historic district. It is, as owner Hank Holliday says, "all things Charleston," and never more so than during an evening celebrating the best of everything.

"Charleston has a unique sense of style," Holliday explains, "one that combines several cultures, that of both the English settlers and the African Americans who built this city and who contributed to the character, texture, and color of this cuisine. In the bustling seventeenth-century colonial seaport, known for its cuisine as much as for its mannerly Southern charm, those cross-cultural currents go way back. "Charleston is thoroughly modern," says Holliday, who was born and raised in the city, before setting out to seek his fortune, "but it preserves the past." On the menu at the inn's Peninsula Grill that means Charleston classics like oyster stew are offered with as much reverence as faraway delicacies that define the good life, including foie gras, the best cuts of salmon, and oysters flown in from Nantucket.

There's an art to preserving the past while embracing the present. As with the grand homes and museums in Charleston's surrounding two-thousand-acre historic district, Planters Inn has withstood fires, floods, hurricanes, and the Civil War. Back in the late eighteenth century, just across the street at the famous City Market, fishermen steered their gigs right into indoor docks, selling fantastically fresh fish. Next to their stalls, others sold livestock and farmers offered their wares. New buildings sprung up around the market, housing beer bottlers, printers, and icehouses, and by the nineteenth century, the cluster of storefronts that would one day become the inn was a dry goods emporium, offering everything from harmonicas and Union suits to petticoats and mousetraps.

Holliday, a self-made financier, has harbored a love of restoration projects since he was a teen working on Nantucket Island, making money during the summers by painting houses there. After starting his own restoration company, then earning a business degree and

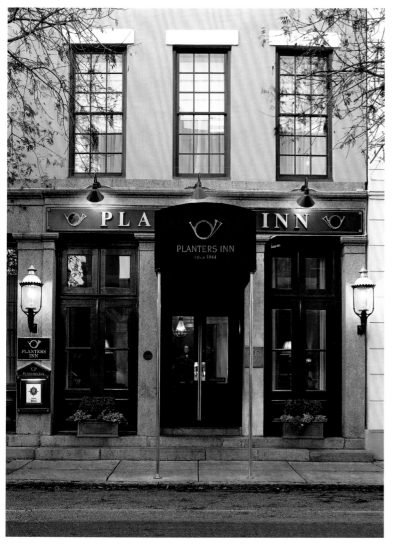

At the heart of old Charleston, Planters Inn occupies a prime location in the city's sprawling historic district but also maintains the local culinary traditions, serving updated classics that include a well-loved succotash and tomato-okra soup. The inn's interiors, designed by Amelia Handegan, reflect a love of Southern classicism, while offering every modern comfort. In the dining room, velvet wall coverings and woven seagrass flooring set the genteel tone.

conquering Wall Street, he found his way back to Charleston, and in 1994 purchased and began painstakingly rehabilitating the inn.

Interpreting the city's current surge of enthusiasm, executive chef Graham Dailey creates an inspiring menu. "The flavors of Charleston are big and bold—butter, bacon, smoke," he says. And who can choose among them? To start the meal, Dailey serves guests a trio of soups, smaller portions of just a few bites each, so that they don't miss a thing. "Most people want to taste it all," he says. "Why limit yourself?" Tonight, the chef's ever-changing selection includes tomato-okra soup, lobster corn chowder, and a velvety-smooth butternut soup topped with candied almonds. "I don't do boring old soup," Dailey says.

With a nod to Charleston's legacy of inimitable seafood, he serves roasted wreckfish on a bed of nouveau succotash, made with baby leeks, sweet corn, and succulent crab, topped with roasted tomato vinaigrette. "In the South, we love succotash with any kind of seafood," he says. "Wreckfish is rich and buttery, and the flavors of the grilled fish with the sweetness of the succotash work so well together." Of course, succotash is something the local clientele is very particular about. "You have to play within certain boundaries. Having grown up with succotash, it's their comfort food," says Dailey, "but visitors to Charleston are excited about it too, having heard so much about succotash." Naturally, many are just as excited to sample the Inn's Planters Punch, with dark rum and a blend of fruit juices.

Dailey offers tender pan-seared scallops as a main course, served with succulent lobster, wilted Bibb lettuce, and whipped chive potatoes. "Our clients are global travelers," says Dailey. "We play with local, but they want to experience the best from around the world, and our scallops are flown in from New England every other day, right off the boat."

There is certainly no better way to end a fabulous Charleston meal than with the wholly local phenomenon known as the Peninsula Grill's Ultimate Coconut Cake, a cherished dessert that can turn any dinner into a celebration. It's a wondrous, towering twelve layers—six of fluffy white cake, six of delectable filling, all topped with cream cheese icing and a gentle flurry of coconut. "It's the cake that ate Charleston," Holliday laughs. Since 1997, founding executive pastry chef Esthi Stefenelli and Peninsula Grill's current executive pastry chef Claire Chapman have refined and revised the recipe, and it's now officially irresistible, selling some dozen or more every day. The dessert even has its own registered federal trademark. "There are days when we've filled the entire cargo bay of a FedEx truck with cake orders being shipped all over the country," Holliday says proudly. "The cake has taken on a life of its own."

Nothing is as timeless as silver and gold. At Planters Inn, the courtyard was decorated with flickering copper carriage lanterns and hundreds of white tea lights—some set afloat in the fountain—while the crepe myrtle trees were wrapped with fairy lights and hung with gilded ornaments. The tabletop was equally alluring, decked out with shimmering gold tablecloths as well as golden plates, mercury glass votives, antique brass candlesticks, and a scattering of walnuts covered in gold foil.

PLANTERS PUNCH

Planters Punch originated in the rum-rich West Indies long ago, but the fresh, fruity cocktail has been a favorite libation in Charleston for more than a century.

MAKES 1 COCKTAIL

1¼ ounces dark rum
1 ounce fresh orange juice
1 ounce pineapple juice
1 teaspoon grenadine syrup
Orange slice
Maraschino cherry

Fill a highball glass with ice and pour in the rum, orange juice, pineapple juice, and grenadine. Stir to combine and garnish with an orange slice and cherry.

ROASTED WRECKFISH WITH LEEK-CRAB SAUTÉ

You've likely tasted Charleston's pristine waters if you've ever ordered wreckfish at a local restaurant. Delicate fish prized for their delicious flavor, wreckfish are caught eight miles offshore of Charleston at the only Atlantic Ocean commercial wreckfish zone. Peninsula Grill serves roasted fillets of this hometown specialty with baby leeks, sweet corn, and crab sauté over grilled asparagus and tomato vinaigrette.

MAKES 4 SERVINGS

Kosher salt and freshly ground black pepper
16 to 20 asparagus spears
6 tablespoons canola oil
1½ cups sliced leeks, white and pale green parts only
1½ cups fresh corn on the cob kernels (2 ears)
6 ounces jumbo lump crabmeat
1 tablespoon diced red bell pepper
1½ tablespoons unsalted butter
2 tablespoons minced fresh chives
4 (6-ounce) wreckfish fillets
½ cup Roasted Tomato Vinaigrette (right)
4 watercress sprigs (optional)

Preheat a grill to high and the oven to 375°F.

Bring a large pot of water and 1 tablespoon salt to a boil. Add the asparagus and cook just until tender, 4 to 6 minutes. Transfer to a bowl filled with ice water to stop the cooking process, then drain.

In a bowl, toss the asparagus with 1 tablespoon of the canola oil, season lightly with salt and pepper, and place on the grill. Cook, turning once, until lightly charred, 2 to 4 minutes per side. Set aside.

Meanwhile, heat 2 tablespoons of the oil in a large skillet over medium-high heat. When the oil is hot, add the leeks and corn and sauté for 2 minutes. Add the crabmeat and cook for 1 minute. Add the bell pepper and cook to warm through, 1 to 2 minutes. Stir in the butter and chives, and season with salt and pepper. Remove from the heat and set aside.

In an ovenproof, nonstick skillet, heat the remaining 3 tablespoons oil over medium-high heat. Season the wreckfish fillets lightly on both sides with salt and pepper. Add the fillets to the pan, flesh side down, and cook until golden brown, about 2 minutes. Turn the fillets over, place the skillet in the oven, and roast until the fish is just cooked through, 4 to 6 minutes.

To plate: Divide the asparagus and leek-crab sauté among 4 plates. Top each plate with a fillet, drizzle with the vinaigrette, and garnish with watercress, if desired.

Roasted Tomato Vinaigrette

MAKES 4 SERVINGS

1 large tomato, quartered
1 teaspoon olive oil
Kosher salt and freshly ground white pepper
1 cup chopped shallots
1 cup chicken stock
½ cup dry white wine
1 garlic clove, crushed
1 teaspoon chopped fresh thyme
2 teaspoons Champagne vinegar
1 cup canola oil

Preheat the oven to 400°F.

Place the tomato on a baking sheet, drizzle with the olive oil, and season lightly with salt and white pepper. Roast until lightly charred, 20 to 25 minutes.

In a medium saucepan, bring the shallots, stock, white wine, garlic, and thyme to a simmer over medium heat. Simmer until the liquid reduces by half, 10 to 15 minutes. Remove the saucepan from the heat and stir in the vinegar and canola oil. Using a blender, puree the roasted tomatoes and the shallot mixture until smooth. Season with salt and white pepper.

PAN-SEARED SCALLOPS WITH
BIBB LETTUCE, LOBSTER, AND CITRUS BROTH

Fresh seafood has played a starring role in Charleston's prized cuisine for more than three centuries. Chef Graham Dailey's delightful pairing of simple greens and succulent scallops is Planters Inn's richly layered salute to Charleston's history.

MAKES 4 SERVINGS

16 large scallops
Kosher salt and freshly ground white pepper
6 tablespoons canola oil
¾ cup (1½ sticks) unsalted butter
1 tablespoon fresh lemon juice
2 heads Bibb lettuce, root ends removed and discarded, chopped
½ pound chopped cooked lobster tail meat
4 cups Whipped Chive Potatoes (right)
Toast Slices (right)
3 tablespoons microgreens (optional)

Season the scallops lightly with salt and white pepper on one side. In a large skillet, heat 3 tablespoons of the canola oil over medium-high heat. When the oil is hot, add 8 of the scallops. Sear until golden brown, 1 to 2 minutes. Turn the scallops over, decrease the heat to medium, and cook until slightly translucent in the center, 4 to 6 more minutes. Repeat with the remaining 3 tablespoons oil and the remaining 8 scallops.

In a medium saucepan, combine 4 cups water with the butter and lemon juice over medium-high heat. Simmer until the liquid reduces by half, 2 to 4 minutes. Stir in the lettuce and lobster meat. Cook until the lettuce is wilted and the lobster is warmed through, 3 to 5 minutes. Remove from the heat and season with salt and white pepper.

To plate: Divide the whipped potatoes among 4 plates, and place 1 or 2 toast slices on top of each serving of potatoes, then top with 3 or 4 scallops. Surround with cooked lettuce and spoon the lobster and broth on top. Garnish with microgreens, if desired.

Whipped Chive Potatoes

MAKES 4 SERVINGS

3 large russet potatoes, peeled and cut into 2-inch pieces
½ cup (1 stick) unsalted butter
1 Vidalia onion, thinly sliced
¼ cup minced fresh chives
½ cup heavy cream
1 tablespoon minced garlic
Kosher salt and freshly ground white pepper

In a medium saucepan, combine the potato pieces and enough water to barely cover. Bring to a boil, decrease the heat to a simmer, and cook until a knife tip easily pierces the potatoes, 10 to 15 minutes. Drain and pass the potatoes through a ricer.

In a large skillet, heat 4 tablespoons of the butter over medium heat. Add the onion and sauté until translucent, 8 to 10 minutes. Using a blender, puree the onion. Add the puree and chives to the riced potatoes. Set aside.

In a small saucepan, combine the remaining 4 tablespoons butter, the cream, and garlic. Bring to a bare simmer over medium heat, then set aside to steep for 1 minute. Pour the butter mixture over the potato mixture, and stir to combine. Season with salt and white pepper.

Toast Slices

MAKES 4 SERVINGS

½ cup (1 stick) unsalted butter
4 slices white bread, halved and crusts removed
Kosher salt and freshly ground white pepper

Preheat the oven to 350°F.

In a medium skillet, melt the butter. Spread the butter on both sides of the bread, season lightly with salt and white pepper, and place on a baking sheet. Toast in the oven, turning once, until golden brown, 4 to 6 minutes per side.

TEA 'TINI

The Planters Inn's signature drink pays homage to drinking tea in Charleston, a tradition that dates back centuries. The cocktail uses freshly squeezed juices for a refreshing twist.

MAKES 1 COCKTAIL

Sugar
1¼ ounces mandarin-flavored vodka
1 ounce favorite sweet tea
½ ounce fresh orange juice
¼ ounce fresh lemon juice
¼ ounce fresh lime juice
Orange twist

Dip the rim of a chilled martini glass into sugar. Combine the vodka, tea, orange juice, lemon juice, and lime juice in a cocktail shaker filled with ice. Shake until chilled and strain into the martini glass. Garnish with an orange twist.

PENINSULA GRILL'S ULTIMATE COCONUT CAKE

Boasting twelve layers of delicious Southern perfection, the Peninsula Grill's signature dessert caused a sensation when it appeared on the restaurant's special Valentine's Day menu in 1997. Truth be told, making the now-iconic cake at home requires both patience and time. If you have neither, remember that Peninsula Grill's pastry team packages whole cakes for delivery across the United States.

MAKES 24 SERVINGS

Coconut Filling
5 cups heavy cream
3 cups sugar
1 pound (4 sticks) unsalted butter
¼ cup cornstarch
1 teaspoon pure vanilla extract
9 cups sweetened shredded coconut

Toasted Coconut Shavings
2 cups sweetened shredded coconut

Cake
Nonstick cooking spray with flour
1 pound (4 sticks) unsalted butter, preferably European style
3 cups sugar

6 large eggs
4½ cups all-purpose flour
1½ tablespoons baking powder
½ teaspoon kosher salt
1½ cups heavy cream
1½ tablespoons pure vanilla extract
1 teaspoon pure coconut extract

Simple Syrup
¾ cup water
¾ cup sugar

Coconut Frosting
1 cup (2 sticks) unsalted butter, at room temperature
8 ounces cream cheese
1 teaspoon pure vanilla extract
1 vanilla bean, scraped
5 cups confectioners' sugar

For the coconut filling: Place the cream, sugar, and butter in a medium saucepan and bring to a boil over medium-high heat, stirring occasionally, until the sugar is dissolved.

Meanwhile, in a small bowl, mix together the cornstarch, vanilla, and 1 tablespoon water. Add to the cream mixture, bring to a boil, and simmer until thickened, about 1 minute.

Place the coconut in the bowl of a food processor. Pulse until the coconut is finely chopped. Remove the cream mixture from the heat and stir in the coconut until well combined. Transfer to a large baking dish and let cool. Cover the filling with plastic wrap and chill overnight.

Just before using, place the filling in the bowl of a stand mixer with the paddle attachment and beat until smooth and creamy, 4 to 5 minutes.

For the toasted coconut shavings: Preheat the oven to 375°F. Line a baking sheet with parchment paper.

Spread the shredded coconut in an even layer on the baking sheet. Bake until golden, 5 to 7 minutes. Set aside to cool.

For the cake: Preheat the oven to 325°F. Spray two 10-inch round cake pans with nonstick cooking spray with flour. Set aside.

In the bowl of a stand mixer with the paddle attachment, cream together the butter and sugar until light and fluffy, 5 to 6 minutes. Add the eggs, one at a time, and beat until creamy, occasionally scraping down the sides of the bowl using a spatula.

In a large bowl, sift together the flour, baking powder, and salt. In a small bowl, mix together the cream, vanilla, and coconut extract. With the mixer on low speed, add the flour mixture to the butter mixture, alternating with the cream mixture and beginning and ending with flour. Beat until just combined.

Pour the batter into the prepared cake pans and bake until a toothpick inserted into the cake comes out clean, 40 to 45 minutes. Let cool completely on a wire rack before removing the cakes from the pans.

For the simple syrup: Combine the water and sugar in a medium saucepan over medium-high heat. Bring to a boil, stirring occasionally, until the sugar has dissolved. Remove from the heat and let cool.

For the coconut frosting: Combine the butter and cream cheese in the bowl of a stand mixer with the paddle attachment and beat until creamy. With the mixer on low speed, slowly add the vanilla extract, the seeds from the vanilla bean, and the confectioners' sugar. Continue beating until smooth and creamy, about 3 minutes.

To assemble: Using a serrated knife, trim the tops of the cakes to make level; discard the trimmings. Cut each cake into 3 even layers. Place 4 strips of parchment paper around the perimeter of a cake plate or lazy Susan.

Place one layer on the cake plate. Brush with about one-fifth of the simple syrup. Spread over 2 cups of the coconut filling. Place a second cake layer on top. Repeat the process with the next 4 layers and top with the remaining layer.

Spread the top and sides of the cake with coconut frosting, keeping in mind you may not need to use all of it. Press the toasted coconut into the sides of the cake. Remove the parchment paper strips.

Chill the cake in the refrigerator for at least 5 hours and up to 5 days. Slice and bring to room temperature before serving.

Southern-Style BRUNCH

GRACIOUS GOOD FOOD, SERVED IN AN ELEGANT AMBIANCE, BRINGS FRIENDS TOGETHER FOR A SOPHISTICATED TAKE ON THE TRADITIONAL SOUTHERN BRUNCH, COMPLETE WITH EVERYONE'S FAVORITE DISHES, BOTH SAVORY AND SWEET.

Bloody Marys   Corn Bread Waffles with Smoked Salmon, Potato Salad, and Horseradish Crème Fraîche
Shrimp and Grits   *Buttermilk Pancakes with Pecans and Caramelized Bananas*
Eggs Benedict with Salmon or Canadian Bacon
Raspberry Tartlets with Almond, Lemon Curd, and Whipped Cream   *Last Word Cocktail*

* RECIPE PROVIDED

Brunch is cheerful, sociable, and inciting," English journalist Guy Beringer wrote in 1895, describing the new midmorning phenomenon in *Hunter's Weekly.* "It is talk-compelling. It puts you in a good temper, it makes you satisfied with yourself and your fellow beings, it sweeps away the worries and cobwebs of the week." Certainly, there is much to be said for the meal that began in aristocratic Britain as a post-hunt breakfast, an alternative to Sunday's heavier after-church lunches, and caught on worldwide. After all, "eliminating the need to get up early on Sunday, brunch would make life brighter for Saturday-night carousers," as Beringer pointed out. Carrying on the tradition at The Fearrington House Inn, a pastoral North Carolinian farm built in 1927, chef Colin Bedford serves traditional Southern brunch fare with all the ebullient sophistication of the meal's origins.

In the American South brunch struck the perfect cord at the turn of the last century, creating an indulgent non-holiday celebration for friends to gather around. In New Orleans, brunching was made popular by German-born restaurateur Madame Bégué. She merged the Bavarian penchant for pre-lunch *brotzeit*, "bread time," when one snacked on a bit of bread, sausage, and beer, with the French love of omelets, coming up with her "second breakfast" in the 1890s, a four-hour feast offering seven courses, all served with coffee and champagne. She treated guests to oysters Rockefeller, pain perdu (what we now call French toast), and eggs Sardou, incorporating spinach and artichokes. Soon enough, eager brunchers boarded riverboat cruises for a deep dive into the meal, as the trend caught on in earnest.

Meanwhile, in New York City, the gilded set enjoyed lavish brunches at the city's best restaurants. On weekends, Emily Post brunched with her female friends at Delmonico's, tucking into oysters, eggs with truffles, and filet mignon. At the Waldorf Astoria in 1894, debonair

The farmhouse at The Fearrington House Inn, wisteria climbing along its eastern trellis, is surrounded by sixty garden beds and offers views of the farm's original dairy house and silo in the distance (opposite). A pristine white table runner, with its dainty faggoted edge and matching soft white napkins, creates a crisp, pretty backdrop, while transparent glass chargers maintain an airy lightness, as do the simplest choices in stemware (see pages 4 and 154).

Wall Street broker Lemeul Benedict proposed a hangover cure to the chef, ordering "buttered toast, poached eggs, crisp bacon, and a hooker of hollandaise." Impressed, Oscar, the restaurant's famous maître d', exchanged ham for bacon and added the dish to the menu. A star was born. (According to Benedict's descendants, he would have loathed the substitution of an English muffin for toast.)

At Fearrington, as the inn's famous Belted Galloways roam their pastures in the distance, guests mill through the homey and tranquil Garden House, full of anticipation. The legendary Edna Lewis once reigned in the kitchen as a guest chef, and a true brunch here showcases the kind of classical Southern dishes she made famous. "A brunch becomes truly 'Southern' when that frame of mind encompasses the meal," says Bedford. "That means hearty ingredients that create a sense of comfort, and conversation that embodies the easygoing and thoughtful attributes of the South."

It all begins with a wonderful riff—savory cornbread waffles served with slivered smoked salmon and horseradish-spiked crème fraîche, sprinkled with pickled mustard seeds. Chef Bedford loves these savory waffles because their flavor doesn't compete with dishes like his shrimp and grits. And while locals know shrimp and grits as a humble everyman's breakfast, Bedford takes the dish to new heights, topping a bowl of smooth grits with fresh shrimp, smoky bacon, and spicy andouille sausage in creamy Parmesan sauce. "Our shrimp and grits recipe pays homage to a tradition, as it is such an iconic dish," says the chef, "but our twist is to add a little Parmesan to finish. The sauce is really what brings it together." Likewise, he updates buttermilk pancakes, serving a fluffy stack decked with pecans and caramelized bananas, the tartness of the buttermilk contrasting so well with the sweet richness of the caramelized fruit. And to Eggs Benedict, the chef's favorite, he adds green onion into the hollandaise sauce. "I love the oozing yolk with the hollandaise," says Bedford, who serves the classic dish two ways, with salmon or with Canadian bacon. (Would old Benedict approve?)

No brunch is complete, however, without its attendant cocktails, and Fearrington's celebration is no exception. The witty Last Word, served in a champagne coup, brings together gin with maraschino liqueur, and yellow chartreuse. It pairs so well with the chef's exquisite raspberry tartlets.

"Breakfast and lunch usually mean you're rushing," says Bedford, "but brunch provides the opportunity to really enjoy food at leisure, savoring the ingredients and the work that went into combining them. There's a sense of relaxation with the meal."

A dainty—yet wonderfully abundant—range of desserts finishes the meal with an indulgent flourish few can resist. Meanwhile, exuberant arrangements of sunny garden flowers, berry-laden branches, and trailing tendrils, most displayed in antique sterling silver vessels, echo the nostalgic and romantically cheerful mood.

CORN BREAD WAFFLES WITH SMOKED SALMON, POTATO SALAD, AND HORSERADISH CRÈME FRAÎCHE

The Fearrington House Inn's chef, Colin Bedford, balances a combination of classic Southern corn bread and potato salad with the sophisticated and dainty addition of smoked salmon and horseradish crème fraîche. The result encompasses everything a Southern brunch should be.

MAKES 8 SERVINGS

Horseradish Crème Fraîche

3 cups sour cream
2 cups heavy cream
1 cup buttermilk
1/4 teaspoon citric acid
Kosher salt and freshly ground black pepper
About 2 teaspoons prepared horseradish
Champagne vinegar

Corn Bread Waffles

1/2 recipe Fearrington House Corn Bread batter (right)

Potato Salad

4 large Yukon gold potatoes, peeled
1/4 cup diced shallots
6 tablespoons olive oil
2 tablespoons sherry vinegar
2 tablespoons maple syrup
1/4 cup chopped fresh herbs
Kosher salt and freshly ground black pepper

Sherry Vinegar Puree

1/4 cup sherry
1/4 cup sherry vinegar
1/4 cup firmly packed brown sugar
2 tablespoons Ultra-Tex 4 (see Notes)

Pickled Mustard Seeds

1/2 cup mustard seeds
1/2 cup dry white wine
1/2 cup white wine vinegar
1/2 cup sugar

To Plate

1 pound smoked salmon, sliced
Celery ribbons (see Notes)
2 cups picked micro herbs, such as celery leaves, chervil, tarragon, watercress, or parsley

For the horseradish crème fraîche: Blend the sour cream, cream, buttermilk, and citric acid by hand and place in a sealed container. Leave overnight in a warm part of your kitchen. After 24 hours, spread the crème fraîche on a clean kitchen towel and let sit for 2 to 3 hours to help pull out any extra moisture. Transfer to a container, season with salt and pepper, and add horseradish to taste and a dash of Champagne vinegar. Refrigerate for up to 3 days.

For the corn bread waffles: Preheat a waffle iron. Add ¾ cup of the corn bread batter to the waffle iron and cook until golden brown. Repeat to make 8 waffles. Don't worry about having perfectly round waffles because they get quartered, and the uneven edges are good for the dish too.

For the potato salad: Bring a pan of salted water to a boil (it should taste like the ocean). Use a small melon baller to scoop out as many balls as possible from the potatoes. Add the balls to the water and cook until fork tender, 4 to 5 minutes. Plunge into ice water to cool. Drain and pat dry with paper towels. Line a rimmed baking sheet with more paper towels, add the potatoes, and roll them around to remove all excess water.

In a large bowl, combine the potatoes with the shallots, olive oil, sherry vinegar, maple syrup, and herbs. Adjust the seasoning with salt and pepper.

For the sherry vinegar puree: Combine the sherry, sherry vinegar, and brown sugar in a small pan and bring to a boil. Remove from the heat and let cool. Sprinkle in the Ultra-Tex while whisking, then allow to sit for a few minutes so the mixture can bloom. If there are too many lumps, you may have to add a little more liquid. Pass through a fine sieve and transfer to a squeeze bottle.

For the pickled mustard seeds: Place the mustard seeds in a pot of cold water and bring to a boil. Drain, then repeat two times, each time starting in cold water. Combine the white wine, white wine vinegar, and sugar in a small pot and bring to a boil. Transfer to a pressure cooker and add the mustard seeds. Cover, bring to pressure, and cook for 25 minutes. (Or cook, covered, in a regular pot on the stove top for about 90 minutes.) Let cool and place in a covered container.

To plate: Cut each waffle into 4 wedges and warm slightly. Shingle the waffle pieces and some smoked salmon pieces down one side of a serving plate. Place a piece of salmon on the other side of the plate and top with a quenelle of horseradish crème fraîche. Spoon two piles of potato salad on either side and arrange celery ribbons and herbs on top. Add a few dots of sherry vinegar puree in the bare areas and then sprinkle the mustard seeds on top.

Notes: Ultra-Tex 4 is a thickener, derived from tapioca, that is available online.

To make celery ribbons, cut a celery rib in half crosswise. Place the celery rib side up and use a peeler to peel the length of the celery, making ribbons. Submerge the ribbons in ice-cold water, preferably overnight, so they curl up.

The Fearrington House Inn Corn Bread

All it takes to conjure childhood memories of a family meal is a well-made corn bread muffin.

Makes 32 muffins

9 ounces gluten-free flour
9 ounces fine yellow cornmeal
1½ teaspoons kosher salt
1½ teaspoons sugar
1 teaspoon baking powder
2½ cups buttermilk
1 cup whole milk
4 large eggs
4 ounces (1 stick) unsalted butter, melted
Chopped fresh chives and parsley, and Parmesan cheese

Combine the flour, cornmeal, salt, sugar, and baking powder in a large bowl. In another bowl, blend by hand the buttermilk, milk, and eggs. Sift the dry ingredients into a separate bowl, then pour in the milk mixture while continuously mixing. Once there are no visible lumps, pour in the butter in a steady stream. Add chives, parsley, and Parmesan to taste.

Use the batter to make the corn bread waffles (left). Or, scoop the batter into 12 well-greased muffin molds. Bake at 350°F for 15 to 20 minutes, until a cake tester inserted into the middle of a muffin comes out clean.

SHRIMP AND GRITS

A Fearrington House Inn classic that withstands the test of time. Simple, yet indulgent, this dish is Southern comfort in a bowl.

MAKES 4 SERVINGS

Parmesan Sauce

2 large onions, sliced
4 garlic cloves, minced
2 to 3 tablespoons vegetable oil
3 cups dry white wine
4 cups heavy cream
1 cup grated Parmesan cheese
Kosher salt and freshly ground black pepper
Grated zest of 1 orange

Grits

1 cup vegetable stock
2 cups whole milk
1/2 large onion, finely diced
2 garlic cloves, minced
2 to 3 tablespoons vegetable oil
1 cup grits
Kosher salt

Shrimp

1/2 cup finely diced red onion
1 cup diced mixed red, yellow, and green bell peppers
2 to 3 tablespoons vegetable oil
8 slices bacon, cooked and chopped
1 cup diced cooked andouille sausage
1/2 cup heavy cream
24 large shrimp, peeled and deveined, tails removed
1/4 cup chopped fresh parsley

To Plate

1/2 cup finely diced tomato
8 scallions, thinly sliced
1/2 cup grated Parmesan cheese

For the Parmesan sauce: In a saucepan over medium heat, sweat the onions and garlic in the vegetable oil until soft and translucent but not browned. Add the white wine, turn the heat to high, and cook until reduced by half. Add the cream and Parmesan and continue to cook until reduced to 4 cups. Puree the sauce in a blender or food processor, working in batches if necessary (see Note).

Pass the sauce through a fine sieve, adjust the seasoning with salt and pepper, and stir in the orange zest. Keep warm until ready to serve; or chill, then gently rewarm before serving.

Note: Do not fill the blender or food processor more than halfway, and be sure the lid is firmly in place to prevent hot liquid from erupting.

For the grits: Bring the stock and milk to a simmer in a saucepan over medium heat. Keep warm.

In a large heavy-bottomed pot (a Dutch oven works well), sweat the onion and garlic in the vegetable oil over medium heat until soft but not browned. Add two-thirds of the hot milk mixture, then whisk in the grits. Lower the heat slightly and cook until the grits are tender (time can vary widely, from 5 minutes for "quick" grits to 40 minutes for stone-ground). If the grits begin to get too thick while cooking, add some of the remaining milk mixture as necessary. Season with salt and keep warm.

For the shrimp: In a saucepan over medium heat, sweat the red onion and bell peppers in the vegetable oil until soft. Add the chopped bacon, andouille, cream, and 3 cups of the Parmesan sauce. Add the shrimp, reduce the heat, and cook just until the shrimp turn pink, about 3 minutes. Stir in the chopped parsley.

To plate: Divide the grits among 4 serving bowls. Spoon the shrimp and bacon cream sauce over the grits, making sure each bowl gets 6 shrimp. Top with the remaining 1 cup Parmesan sauce. Garnish with diced tomato, scallions, and grated Parmesan. Serve immediately.

LAST WORD COCKTAIL

A classy cocktail, served in old-fashioned barware, is a timeless pairing for any meal, and delightful when matched with desserts.

MAKES 1 COCKTAIL

½ ounce gin
½ ounce fresh lime juice
½ ounce maraschino liqueur
½ ounce yellow chartreuse
Lime slice

In a cocktail shaker with ice, combine the gin, lime juice, maraschino liqueur, and chartreuse. Strain into a Champagne coupe and garnish with a lime slice.

RASPBERRY TARTLETS WITH ALMOND, LEMON CURD, AND WHIPPED CREAM

Every brunch needs a classic, and Fearrington House Inn's tartlets are sweet and tangy, just like the conversations held at a ladies' afternoon brunch. Chef Colin Bedford's combination of fruit and whipped cream is enhanced by the nutty flavors of the almond crust and the citrus notes of the lemon curd.

MAKES 8 SERVINGS

Almond Dough

6.3 ounces unsalted butter
5 ounces confectioners' sugar
1.75 ounces almond flour
1 large egg plus 1 large egg yolk, lightly beaten
3.2 ounces all-purpose flour
9.5 ounces cake flour

Almond Cream

8.8 ounces unsalted butter
8.8 ounces sugar
0.9 ounce all-purpose flour
3 large eggs
8.8 ounces almond flour

Lemon Curd

1 cup fresh lemon juice
7 large egg yolks
3 large whole eggs
5.3 ounces sugar
5.3 ounces cold unsalted butter, diced

Stabilized Whipped Cream

1/2 teaspoon powdered gelatin
1 cup heavy cream
1 ounce sugar

To Bake and Assemble

1/2 cup raspberry jam
2 half pints raspberries
1 half pint blueberries
Confectioners' sugar
White chocolate curls

For the almond dough: Cream the butter and confectioners' sugar in a stand mixer with the paddle attachment until pale white. Add the almond flour. Once the flour is incorporated, pour in the beaten egg and yolk in a steady stream. Once thoroughly mixed in, add the all-purpose flour and then the cake flour.

As soon as the flour is incorporated, stop the mixer. Remove the dough and shape into a ball. Then wrap the dough in plastic wrap. Refrigerate for 4 to 6 hours or up to 2 days.

For the almond cream: Use the stand mixer with the paddle attachment and beat the butter and sugar until pale in color. Add the all-purpose flour and eggs. Lastly, mix in all of the almond flour. Place in a container and refrigerate for 4 to 6 hours, or up to 2 days. Remove from the fridge about 30 minutes before using and place in a piping bag.

For the lemon curd: Combine the lemon juice, egg yolks, whole eggs, and sugar in a saucepan. Heat over medium heat, whisking continuously, until the mixture begins to bubble. Remove from the heat and mix in the cold butter until melted. Strain, pour into a shallow container, and press plastic wrap directly on top of the lemon curd. Refrigerate for at least 6 hours, but the lemon curd is better when made the day before so it can chill overnight.

For the whipped cream: Soak the gelatin in 1/2 tablespoon ice water for 5 minutes. Warm the cream over low heat to about 122°F, which is just enough to melt the sugar and gelatin. Add the sugar and gelatin and beat by hand until soft peaks form. Refrigerate overnight.

To bake the tartlets: Preheat the oven to 325°F.

Roll out the almond dough to about 1/4 inch thick and cut out eight 6-inch circles. You can reroll the dough once, but allow it to chill for 30 minutes before doing so. Line eight 3 1/2- to 4-inch rings with the dough rounds.

Divide the raspberry jam among the tarts, spreading it evenly across the bottoms. Using a piping bag, pipe on the almond cream in a spiral motion. Bake until golden brown, 25 to 30 minutes. Allow to cool in the rings for at least 1 hour to reach room temperature (a suitable temperature so the lemon curd does not melt). Then remove from the rings.

To assemble: Spoon some of the lemon curd on top of each tartlet. Using the back of the spoon in a circular motion, swirl, leaving 1/2 inch around the outside of the tart. Position the raspberries and blueberries on top of the tart. Add dots of whipped cream and garnish with confectioners' sugar and white chocolate curls.

HOW TO CREATE THE PERFECT HARVEST CENTERPIECE

———

Mary Stevens, Fearrington's principal floral designer since 2001, was inspired by a silver bowl, which was, in fact, an antique bread basket, when creating the morning's masterful arrangements. Using the bowl as her central container, she surrounded it with smaller arrangements done in vintage silver julep cups. Each container was lined with a plastic bag, in order to protect the metal from water. Stevens then placed a floral frog in each base. Using floral tape, she created a grid across the top of each container, to keep any flowers from wandering.

From the property's cutting garden, she selected a variety of seasonal flowers, as well as charming bunches of rosemary and ornamental kale. Hydrangea blooms and magnolia foliage, her most "visually heavy" items, gave the arrangement its foundation, while also hiding the frog and florist's tape.

Next she built up layer upon layer of other blooms, incorporating roses, grouping them in threes, as well as bittersweet vines, clematis, ranunculus, and craspedia. "Keep the arrangement interesting by incorporating different textures, colors, and sizes," she suggests. "Allow the natural line of each stem to work in the overall gracefulness of the arrangement." Smaller items have more impact when grouped together, she notes, and the overall height of the display should allow for seated guests to easily see one another over it. "The last 'rule' is that there aren't any," Stevens concludes. "Once you're happy with your final arrangement, you are all done."

Smoky Mountains
DINNER

AT BLACKBERRY FARM UTTER DEVOTION TO LOCAL FOODWAYS
CREATES A GLORIOUS MENU, AND NEVER MORE SO THAN AT HARVEST TIME,
WHEN THE CROPS—AND THE KITCHEN—REACH NEW HEIGHTS.

The Oak Tree Cocktail*   *Cheese and Charcuterie Board**   *Sea Island Red Peas**
Roasted Mushrooms*   *Roasted Carrots**   *Creamy Corn Grits**
Roasted Beet Salad with Brebis Cheese and Pecans   *Wood-Roasted Rack of Lamb**

* RECIPE PROVIDED

L ong before farm-to-table was a dining trend, it was a way of life at Blackberry Farm, the old stone and clapboard Tennessee manor that Kreis and Sandy Beall purchased as their family home in 1976, raising their son Sam there and converting the place into a small inn several years later. Nestled into a verdant stretch of the Smoky Mountains, visitors to the bucolic spot can't help but use words like "authentic" and "genuine," when they find themselves so deeply immersed in the family's passion for the customs, culture, and foodways of the Smoky Mountains foothills.

The Bealls' fascination with the local cuisine put Blackberry Farm at the forefront of the Southern cooking movement, with the renowned kitchen serving meals that celebrate the kind of "homey, soul-satisfying, belly-filling food that takes the best and freshest foods of the season and puts them on our plates," as one reviewer wrote. Working in accord with the natural rhythms of the land, the Bealls' approach is ultra-artisanal, incorporating some 110 varieties of vegetables grown on the farm, as well as the precious products created in Blackberry's own creamery, preservation kitchen, charcuterie shop, and brewery. "It's such a large palette to work from and it's so much fun to have that variety at your fingertips," says chef Cassidee Dabney. "Sometimes I have to pinch myself."

All that historic relevance—and reverence—appears as a delicious spread on the table when friends gather for a cozy farm dinner out in the Yallerhammer, an open-air pavilion built around a huge stacked stone fireplace. The view is breathtaking, as the fields spread out into a corridor of green and the sounds of a rushing brook hover in the smoky air. Out on an iron table grill, chef Dabney is roasting a rack of lamb over a glowing bank of hickory and oak coals. "I love the craftsmanship of cooking over wood, which is such a dynamic heat source, imparting a different flavor characteristic depending on the type of wood you use, or whether it's wet or dry," she says. "There are so many variables."

As night falls, a warm glow emanates from the Yallerhammer, an open-air pavilion built around a stacked stone hearth, and the air is rich with woodsmoke wafting from the chef's hickory and oak coals. Nestled into the foothills of the Smoky Mountains, Blackberry Farm is at the forefront of the revival in Southern cuisine. Cherished local dishes are crafted nightly in the renowned kitchen, where the chef is supplied with every rare artisanal ingredient, including those grown and made on site.

Cooking with smoke and fire has also been a longtime fascination at Blackberry Farm, which is equipped with every kind of cooker, and where everyone in the kitchen learns the art of regulating smoke and air to achieve the best flavor. In the foothills, many homes didn't have cookstoves until the turn of the nineteenth century. Open-hearth cooking is essential to the local cuisine, as is that unmistakable taste of smoke.

On the burlap-covered tables, antique jars and butter crocks full of flowers cut on the property—from morning glories to cockscomb and daisies to hearts-a-bustin'—look right at home. A tantalizing cheese board boasts award winners from the farm creamery, made from milk supplied by its sheep. From the larder comes a variety of salumi and charcuterie, all harvested from the farm's hogs. The creamy grits were crafted from two nineteenth-century heirloom corn varieties of Hickory King corn and Pencil Cob, both milled and ground down just so, just as the Sea Island red peas, roasted mushrooms, and roasted carrots all come from the land. "In the foothills, people have lived on rugged terrain under challenging conditions, with such extreme seasons," says Dabney. "Blackberry Farm's Foothills Cuisine is about finding a way to use every little bit of anything, which is such a creative and exciting way to take advantage of what's here, and all the flavors that are possible."

Through alliances with the region's most knowledgeable historians, Blackberry Farm is devoted to preserving and celebrating local traditions of every sort. Truffles are sought out in the fall, and in the spring Shannon Walker, the farm's preservationist, forages for the kitchen, ranging the valley on the farm's behalf. John Coykendall, a local legend and agricultural expert, rigorously attends to the farm plantings, overseeing the endless rows of Cherokee Cornfield and Turkey Craw beans and Piggott peas. There's talk of dipper gourds and ham smoking, and the state of the hazelnut trees. And, to be sure, the food that comes from the farm's kitchen—from pickled ramps to the rustic blueberry tart—tastes of the wisdom of generations.

They say that at dawn and at dusk the shadows draped over these mountains are more pronounced, especially in autumn, when the smoky veil hanging near the ridgeline truly looks blue. Leaves tumble by on the fall breeze, and as the inky night falls, several guests wrap their shoulders in blankets thoughtfully hung on the backs of their chairs. But the traditional bluegrass Misty River band is just warming up. You could say that it's a very Tennessee moment.

An array of antique stoneware jugs and crockery captures the homey, nostalgic mood, especially when filled with all sorts of old-fashioned blooms from the garden, including a variety of daisies, allium, marigolds, dahlias, freesia, and native hearts-a-bustin'. Rustic ceramic plates in earth tones contrast with elaborately monogrammed white napkins, each boasting an intricately serpentine "BF"—for Blackberry Farm, of course.

The evening's cheese and charcuterie plate showcased the glories of the local terroir, with finocchiona, soppressata, and Toscano salami, from Blackberry Farm's own charcuterie shop, as well as Singing Brook, Appalachian Gold, and Little Ewe cheeses from its creamery. The spread also included the farm's highly coveted pickled ramps, bread-and-butter pickles, and strawberry-ramp jam, crafted on site in the preservation kitchen. As the old Appalachian saying goes, "First you eat all you can from your garden, then you can what you can't eat." A large selection of these wares is available for sale through the farm catalog, which also offers heirloom seeds to grow your own Pencil Cob corn or brown crowder field peas.

THE OAK TREE

Blackberry Farm's signature cocktail starts rich and warm with a subtle vanilla and spice from bourbon and maple syrup, then finishes with bright citrus and balance from the vermouths, orange peel, and bitters.

MAKES 1 COCKTAIL

2 ounces Ancient Age Kentucky Straight Bourbon Whiskey
½ ounce Dolin Vermouth de Chambéry Rouge (sweet)
½ ounce Dolin Vermouth de Chambéry Blanc
1 bar spoon Pappy & Company Bourbon Barrel-Aged Pure
  Maple Syrup
2 dashes of Fee Brothers Old Fashion Aromatic Bitters
Orange peel

Put ice in a rocks glass and add the bourbon, rouge vermouth, blanc vermouth, maple syrup, and bitters. Stir for 45 seconds, until very cold and thoroughly mixed. Rim the glass with an orange peel and drop it into the glass.

In the open-air pavilion, each chair is hung with a soft blanket—a thoughtful touch, as in the foothills the temperatures drop rapidly when the sun goes down. Outside, chef Cassidee Dabney works over an iron table grill. "We love cooking over an open flame," she says. "It's sensory overload to walk past meat roasting over an open flame—the smoke, the flames, the rich smell—amazing." The smoky taste makes a perfect counterpoint to the award-winning, light and refreshing beer Saison, crafted in the Blackberry Farm Brewery.

SEA ISLAND RED PEAS

Blackberry Farm sources Sea Island red peas from South Carolina producer Anson Mills. The heirloom field pea is robust in flavor and creamy in texture. Black-eyed peas would make a worthy substitution if Sea Island peas are unavailable.

MAKES 4 TO 6 SERVINGS

1 cup Sea Island red peas
8 cups vegetable stock or water
1 sachet of fresh thyme sprigs, fresh parsley sprigs, and a
*   bay leaf tied in a bundle with butcher's twine*
1 small carrot
1 celery rib
1/2 onion
Kosher salt
Mint Chimichurri (below)

Soak the peas in 2 quarts water overnight.

Drain the peas and place in a pot with the stock and sachet. Bring to a boil, reduce to a slow simmer, and cook until the peas are almost tender, 30 to 45 minutes. Add the carrot, celery, and onion and continue to simmer until the peas are tender, 10 to 15 minutes longer. Season with salt and cool in the liquid.

Remove the sachet and vegetables and drain any excess liquid. Fold in about half of the chimichurri. (Save the leftover chimichurri to serve with grilled lamb.)

Mint Chimichurri

MAKES ABOUT 2 CUPS

1 teaspoon kosher salt
2 cups fresh mint leaves
2 cups fresh parsley leaves
1 shallot, chopped
1 teaspoon chopped garlic
1/2 cup garlic oil (see Note)
About 1/4 cup red wine vinegar

Dissolve the salt in 1 cup hot water and let cool. Chop together the mint, parsley, shallot, and garlic. Transfer to a bowl and add the salted water and garlic oil. Add the vinegar to taste.

Note: To make garlic oil, combine the peeled cloves of 2 heads of garlic with 1/2 cup olive oil and 1/2 cup canola oil in a heavy pan. Gently roast in a 300°F oven for about 50 minutes, until the garlic is soft. Drain the garlic cloves (use them on bread, in dressings, et cetera) and use the flavored oil in place of olive oil.

ROASTED MUSHROOMS

The farm likes to spoon a tangle of roasted mushrooms alongside many of their entrées. Look for interesting mushroom varieties at your local farmers' market, or enjoy the simplicity of the humble yet delicious button mushroom.

MAKES 4 TO 6 SERVINGS

4 cups mushrooms, such as oysters, hen of the woods,
*   or buttons, trimmed*
4 tablespoons vegetable oil
2 fresh thyme sprigs
2 tablespoons sherry vinegar
Kosher salt

Cut or pull apart the mushrooms into bite-size pieces.

Heat a large skillet over high heat. Add 2 tablespoons of the vegetable oil to the very hot pan, followed by half of the mushrooms. Toss the mushrooms in the pan to coat with oil, then cook, without turning the mushrooms too much so that they can brown nicely, until one side is golden brown, 4 to 6 minutes. Flip the mushrooms, add 1 thyme sprig, and transfer to a large bowl. Repeat with the remaining mushrooms, oil, and thyme. Stir the sherry vinegar into the mushrooms and toss, then season with salt.

ROASTED CARROTS

So simple and so sweet.

MAKES 4 TO 6 SERVINGS

25 baby carrots, trimmed and cleaned
1/2 cup grape seed oil
4 fresh thyme sprigs
Kosher salt and freshly ground black pepper

Preheat the oven to 400°F.

In a large bowl, toss the carrots with the grape seed oil, thyme, and salt and pepper. Place the carrots on a baking sheet and roast for 10 to 15 minutes, until tender.

CREAMY CORN GRITS

Blackberry Farm grows its own Hickory King corn, an heirloom variety that is prized for its huge yellow kernels and that makes excellent grits. The fresh-ground grits typically take a very long time to cook: Chef Cassidee Dabney notes that the slower you cook the grits and the more often you stir them, the creamier they will be.

MAKES 4 TO 6 SERVINGS

2 cups vegetable stock
2 cups whole milk
2 tablespoons kosher salt
1 cup fresh-ground corn grits, sifted with the germ removed
Unsalted butter

In a heavy pot, bring the stock, milk, and salt to a boil. Slowly whisk the grits into the boiling stock. Cook, stirring constantly, until thickened, about 10 minutes. Reduce the heat to low and slowly cook the grits, stirring often to avoid sticking or scorching, for 4 to 5 hours, until tender with only a slight bite. Season to taste and finish with a generous spoonful of fresh butter.

WOOD-ROASTED RACK OF LAMB

Blackberry Farm's chef Dabney says she loves the sweet gamy earthiness of lamb; it is a perfect complement to smoke and fresh Smoky Mountains night air.

MAKES 4 SERVINGS

1 cup grape seed oil
4 garlic cloves, minced
2 tablespoons chopped fresh rosemary
1 large rack of lamb, frenched
Kosher salt and freshly ground black pepper

Mix together the grape seed oil, garlic, and rosemary. Rub the mixture on the rack of lamb and then season liberally with salt and pepper. Set aside.

Start a small fire using split hickory logs (about 6) and allow the wood to burn until the logs are completely charred and starting to carbonize. Spread the logs and embers and set a grill grate about 1 foot above the fire. Allow the grill grate to become hot.

Place the lamb, fat side down, on the grill over the coals and sear. (The rendering lamb fat might cause the fire to flame up; if this happens, remove the lamb and allow the flame up to pass.) Flip the rack to the other side and move to a cooler area of the grill. Slowly roast the rack, turning often to ensure even cooking, for 10 to 12 minutes, until a meat thermometer inserted into the thickest part of the rack registers 135° to 140°F. Remove the lamb from the grill and let rest for 5 to 10 minutes. Slice the rack into chops and serve immediately.

Halloween COSTUME PARTY

CASTING HIS SPELL, THE EXTRAORDINARY CHEF PATRICK O'CONNELL
SHARES A LOVE OF OPULENT FANTASY, OFFERING GUESTS A
FAIRY-TALE EVENING FULL OF SURPRISES—BOTH BREATHTAKINGLY
MARVELOUS AND DOWNRIGHT MACABRE.

*The Wicked Witch's Apple**   *Beef Heart Skewers with Shishito Peppers*
Bloody Mary Gelées   *"Eyeball" Blini with Caviar*   *Squash Risotto with Chanterelles**
*Bison Short Ribs with Red Beet Puree**   *Dessert Tray*

* RECIPE PROVIDED

A great meal can provide sustenance, respite, even inspiration, but only very rarely does it deliver transformation. However, Patrick O'Connell, the extraordinary chef and creative force behind The Inn at Little Washington, is a master of merging fantasy with reality, a state he likes to call "fantality." While the glorious everyday fantality chez O'Connell might fall somewhere midway between the two states, at Halloween the marker takes a giant leap toward the fantastical. With his heart set on creating a carnivalesque "European take on All Hallow's Eve," O'Connell transports the notion of an autumnal costume party into a whole new realm, one that reorients the senses with sumptuous food, decadent indulgences, and thrilling sights to behold.

Preparing for the evening, the chef took his cues, more specifically, from Europe of the eighteenth century, when Venetian aristocrats spent nearly half the year—October through Lent—cloaked, hooded, and masked, deliriously flocking from one celebration to another. In Paris, Louis XIV insisted on universal disguising at his royal balls, and was seen in court ballets performing as a bacchante, shepherd, and nymph. In rollicking London, midnight masquerades drew eccentrically costumed partiers done up as harlequins, demons, and witches, with one of the queen's maids of honor dressed as a bare-breasted Iphigenia, and George II and the Prince of Wales lost among the throngs. As an anonymous writer explained in an English magazine of the era, "a masquerade is one of the most entertaining diversions that ever was imported; you may hear and see, and do everything in the world, without the least reserve—and liberty, liberty, my dear, you know, is the very joy of my heart."

Joyous Anonymous isn't the only one who loves to let loose. By importing that sense of freewheeling abandon, scented with a wanton hint of debauchery, O'Connell "allowed guests to channel someone from a bygone age," he says. "It creates a surreal aspect that's fun to

Far from the cold-edged aesthetic favored by some, chef and inn owner Patrick O'Connell takes inspiration from great master paintings of centuries past. "When you see work by court painters like Velázquez, their work is so layered and luscious," he explains. O'Connell's setting is just as theatrically vibrant, whether he's arranged for a footman in a tricorn hat to greet party guests arriving by horse-drawn carriage or has overseen the placement of a sky-scraping croquembouche among the picturesque bowls of fruit and antique porcelains. Meanwhile, dramatic candlesticks tower over swags of seasonal foliage tumbling from the mantelpiece.

play with." The topsy-turvy attitude was reflected in the evening's menu, full of surprises, including grilled beef heart skewers with shishito peppers and a romanesco dipping sauce, all served with a devilishly good new cocktail called The Wicked Witch's Apple.

But then, O'Connell has exercised his freedom to dream big ever since 1978, when he and his former partner Reinhardt Lynch opened their restaurant in the tiny country town of Washington, Virginia, renting half of a former auto repair shop. A humble start, to be sure, but O'Connell's tastes run toward the epic, and these days his whimsical world includes not only the restaurant, but an inn of twenty-four guest rooms, as well as boutiques, a ball-room, and sprawling gardens that make a whole campus of opulently appointed buildings—their rich, theatrical interiors designed by London's legendary Joyce Conwy Evans—spread throughout the unspoiled colonial village.

"We offer an antidote to hard-edged reality," says O'Connell, "an escape from the nasti-ness of modern life. There are so many passions playing out. There's almost nothing like it in this country." To be sure, actualizing O'Connell's monumental vision has meant eschewing shortcuts. "We don't think in half measures," he says with a wry laugh. It makes for a stirring ambiance. "The intention with our decor is that you would never bore. I think that's the hall-mark of a great interior," he continues. "It makes you smile—you can't restrain it—and you know that the person who created the space enjoyed themselves."

Clearly, O'Connell enjoys these creations immensely. Costumed party guests arrive by horse-drawn carriage and wend their way into the living room to sample blinis served with caviar (to look like eyes). O'Connell is their theatrical director, stalking his set, scrutinizing his players, searching for flaws in the facade. "We strove to bring the space to life in the man-ner of a film or stage set," he says. "At first glance you saw one thing, then with another glance, another layer."

Before becoming a chef, O'Connell had thought about becoming an actor, but found what he called the "living theater" of the restaurant more compelling. Still, when describing his work, he likens cuisine to music (noting the harmonies in each dish) or to painting. "I look to fine art and great painters like Velázquez for inspiration," he says. "Their work is so layered and luscious. They draw you in." If each meal he creates looks like a still life wor-thy of the greats, then his blue-and-white kitchen, inspired by the dairy room at Windsor Castle, makes an especially fine gallery, with its hanging lanterns, Portuguese painted tiles, and baronial fireplace. There, revelers dine on squash risotto with chanterelles "served in-side a gorgeous hollowed roasted pumpkin, which keeps it perfectly warm," says O'Connell.

Helping guests feel at ease with a costume party means letting them in on the inspiration and narrowing the parameters a bit. Patrick O'Connell specifically asked his guests to channel a European All Hallow's Eve masque of the eighteenth century, which "created a surreal aspect that's fun to play with," he says. "They could appear as someone from a bygone era."

Beef short ribs are served with a beet puree. Then, with otherworldly perfection, out come the dainty maple pecan swans swimming over a delicate silver stand. "We regard every detail of what we do with complete consciousness and bring a precision to all that we're trying to convey," O'Connell says.

Occasionally, in fact, the chef invites the director of the Washington Ballet and his ballerinas to come train the restaurant staff, and the two groups take turns escorting each other to the tables. Taken to this extreme, the exercise makes it easy to see how "the staff played to the space and the space became more than it seemed," O'Connell says. "The expertise of a male dancer is to make the female appear more than she is, as if she were truly capable of supporting herself on one toe, whereas in reality he holds her weight." "It's all in how she's being received," O'Connell concludes. "And that's what we do every night. Guests feel they're more than they are."

THE WICKED WITCH'S APPLE

This elegant cocktail combines some of our favorite flavors
of fall and will sweep you away to an enchanted place.

MAKES 1 COCKTAIL

1 lemon wedge
2 tablespoons sugar mixed with a pinch of ground cinnamon
1 ounce Laird's Apple Brandy
3/4 ounce Strega liqueur
3/4 ounce My Amaro liqueur
1/2 ounce pear puree
1 ounce cold sparkling apple cider
2 fresh apple slices
2 kirsch-soaked cherries (available in gourmet stores and online)

Run the lemon across the rim of a classic Champagne coupe
or martini glass. Roll the rim in the cinnamon sugar.

Combine the apple brandy, Strega, amaro, and pear puree in
a cocktail shaker with ice. Shake quickly to combine and strain
into the sugar-rimmed glass. Add a splash of cider.
Garnish with apple slices and cherries.

An early fascination with fairy tales led Patrick O'Connell to the kitchen,
where, for this fête, he crafted an evocatively eerie range of delights,
including skewers of grilled beef heart and shishito peppers, served with
romanesco sauce, Bloody Mary gelées, and trompe l'oeil blinis, designed
to look like roving eyes. It was all witty and wondrous—and perfectly
in keeping with the dinner's decadently ghoulish theme. "The opulence
of our set brought to mind a masque." he says.

SQUASH RISOTTO WITH CHANTERELLES

The velvety texture of the Inn at Little Washington's risotto is heightened by the addition of a seasonal squash puree. Toasted pecans enhance the natural elements of fall. The inn serves the risotto in a striking roasted pumpkin hollowed "bowl."

MAKES 5 TO 6 SERVINGS

Risotto Base

3 tablespoons minced shallots
1 tablespoon minced garlic
1 tablespoon unsalted butter
1 pound Carnaroli or Arborio rice
1/2 bottle (3/4 cup) dry white wine
About 6 cups chicken stock, as needed

Squash Puree

1 red kuri squash, halved, seeded, and flesh cut into large dice
1/2 cup (1 stick) unsalted butter
1/4 cup pure maple syrup
3 tablespoons sherry vinegar
Kosher salt
1 small bunch fresh thyme sprigs
1 tablespoon fennel seeds
1 tablespoon whole cloves

To Plate

1 cup sliced fresh chanterelles
Unsalted butter as needed
1 tablespoon minced candied ginger
Freshly grated nutmeg
Calvados as needed
Chicken stock
Grated Parmesan cheese as needed
Kosher salt and freshly ground white pepper
Brown butter–toasted pecans as needed
Microgreens, such as radish, kale, or tatsoi, as needed

For the risotto base: In a heavy saucepan over medium heat, sweat the shallots and garlic in the butter. Add the rice and cook, stirring, until the rice sounds like pebbles and dries out. Add the white wine and cook down until almost gone, stirring frequently.

Add enough stock to cover the rice. Simmer until the liquid is absorbed and the rice is tender but still al dente, about 30 minutes. (You may need one or two more additions of stock to cook the rice to the desired texture.) Spread the rice thinly on a baking sheet and cool rapidly in the refrigerator. (The risotto base can be made in advance, kept in the refrigerator for a few days, and finished in only a few minutes.)

For the squash puree: Preheat the oven to 350°F.

Place the diced squash in a roasting pan and season with the butter, maple syrup, sherry vinegar, and salt. Add the thyme, fennel seeds, and cloves, then pour 1/4 inch of water into the bottom of the pan. Cover the pan with aluminum foil and bake for 1 hour, or until the squash is tender. Remove and discard the thyme sprigs and cloves. In batches if necessary, puree the squash in a blender until smooth. Pass the puree through a chinois to strain, adjust the seasoning if necessary, and reserve.

To plate: In a large heavy sauté pan, sear the chanterelles in 1 tablespoon butter until lightly colored. Add the candied ginger and nutmeg to taste and a couple teaspoons of Calvados.

Add the cooked rice and about 1 cup of the squash puree, and heat through. Adjust the texture with stock: You are looking for a loose and creamy, but not soupy, consistency. If the rice is too thick, thin with stock, but remember that you are still adding Parmesan and butter to finish, which will loosen up the risotto. Over medium-low heat, *mount* the risotto by gradually stirring in about 1/2 cup butter and 1 cup Parmesan until the risotto is smooth and luxurious. Adjust the seasoning with additional Calvados, squash puree, nutmeg, salt, and pepper. Garnish with brown butter–toasted pecans and microgreens.

BISON SHORT RIBS WITH RED BEET PUREE

There are not many things more warming than braised beef and vegetables on a cold wintery day. The Inn at Little Washington's take is heightened by utilizing grass-fed bison, earthy beets, and sweet pomegranate juice.

MAKES 4 TO 6 SERVINGS

Bison Short Ribs

2 pounds bison short ribs
Kosher salt and freshly ground black pepper
1 tablespoon grape seed oil
2 organic carrots, cut into large dice
1 sweet onion, cut into large dice
2 garlic cloves
2 quarts beef stock
1/4 teaspoon cayenne pepper
1/4 teaspoon paprika
1/2 teaspoon garlic powder

Beet Puree

1/2 pound red beets
2 cups pomegranate juice
1 tablespoon unsalted butter
Kosher salt and freshly ground black pepper

To Plate

Fried onion rings (optional)
Microgreens

For the bison short ribs: Preheat the oven to 325°F.

With a sharp boning knife, remove all silver skin from the short ribs. Season generously with salt and pepper. In a large heavy pot over medium-high heat, heat the grape seed oil. Once the oil slightly smokes, carefully add the seasoned short ribs, in batches if necessary, and sear on all sides, until dark brown and caramelized. Remove the ribs and reserve on the side. (Leave all caramelized bits in the bottom of the pot.)

Add the carrots and onion to the pot and sear on all sides until light brown and caramelized. Add the garlic cloves and return the reserved bison to the pot. Add the stock, cayenne, paprika, and garlic powder and bring the mixture to a simmer. Cover the pot with a lid and transfer to the oven. Slowly cook the short ribs for 3 hours, or until tender. Season with salt and black pepper.

Meanwhile, for the beet puree: Peel and cut the beets into large pieces. In a medium heavy pot, add the beets and cover with the pomegranate juice. Cook over low heat until the beets are tender, about 30 to 40 minutes. Remove the beets and keep warm.

Over high heat, reduce the pomegranate juice to about 1/2 cup and a syrupy consistency.

In a blender, combine the cooked beets, pomegranate reduction, and butter. Blend on high until smooth. Season with salt and black pepper. (Makes about 2 cups.)

To plate: Place a spoonful of beet puree on each plate. Using the back of the spoon, smear the puree to create a thin layer for the ribs to sit on. Place the short ribs over the beet puree and garnish with fried onion rings, if you like, and microgreens.

A bevy of sweets to die for: The range included tiny lemon tartlets topped with a delicate mound of fresh raspberries, classic macarons, curls of candied grapefruit rind, pecan cookie swans, orange shortbread, and miniature cream puffs with caramel. The pièce de résistance, however, was miniature candied apples, dipped in caramel spiked with bourbon, which were "so pretty all rolled in different toppings," says the chef, "nuts or chocolate or sprinkles, each one different."

Autumn Colors CELEBRATION

SURROUNDED BY LAKESIDE VISTAS OF TREMENDOUS BEAUTY,
AND SATIATED BY EXCEPTIONALLY CREATIVE CUISINE, GUESTS SAVOR AN
ALFRESCO EVENING EXPRESSING THE REGION'S NATURAL WONDERS.

*Mouzette Cocktail**   *Caramelized Apples**   *Squash Gnocchi with Deer Jerky*
*Swordfish Cru with Pine Mushrooms, Celtuce, and Sea Lettuce**
*Red Deer Loin with Beets, Onion Reduction, Romanesco, and Sea Rocket Berries**
Sweet Clover Chocolate Cake   *Manoir Hovey's Chocolate Landscape**

* RECIPE PROVIDED

In Quebec, autumn ignites the senses with fresh flavors and a spectacular array of fiery foliage. It's a season when "the Maples blaze out in scarlet," as American naturalist Henry David Thoreau put it in 1863, when the great yellowed elms brighten the sky and when visitors to the Northeast marvel at the "red tents of the Oaks, which on each side are mingled with the liquid green of the Pines." At Manoir Hovey, a glorious inn built in 1900 on the banks of Lake Massawippi, guests revel in this season of seasons, gathering for a warming dinner of fascinating seasonal food out on the end of a long wooden dock, surrounded by the dark tranquil waters and a burnished halo of birch.

Thoreau's legendary love of nature turned him into a renegade, and with a remarkably innovative spirit chef Francis Wolf expresses a similar passion for the forest surrounding Manoir Hovey. His hyper-localized take on Quebecois cuisine utilizes flavors that are utterly unique, originating in an array of exquisite ingredients foraged directly from the woods. "We try to use everything the forest has available," he says.

The chef, who grew up in the area, began his quest at twelve, when a hunting trip with his father first hinted at his future profession and passion. Learning to clean and cook a hare instilled a respect for the forest's wild bounty, but it also piqued his young imagination. "I began to dream of all the ways that food can be transformed," Wolf remembers. "I'm pretty sure I'll never stop dreaming about food." Eventually, after apprenticing in Quebec, and honing his skills in New York's top kitchens, under chefs like Alain Ducasse, Daniel Boulud, and Charlie Palmer, Wolf returned to Canada and has been at Manoir Hovey for the past twelve years.

With his inventive approach, using unusual ingredients specific to the place—from beach rose hips to sea buckthorn—chef Wolf expresses the flavor of Quebec in a whole new way. His kitchen is bursting with wild herbs and fragrant wild mushrooms, as well as locally raised livestock such as goat calf, highland veal and beef, and Quebec's fabulous duck and foie gras.

Autumn, when foliage turns the landscape to Technicolor and when the swollen-stalked mushrooms are in season, is a perfect time to visit Manoir Hovey. Dining formally at an elegantly appointed table on the dock is an utterly transcendent experience, from the carved pumpkin lanterns to the adventurous meal expressing the local landscape through novel ingredients foraged in the surrounding woods.

"Several of the cooks here are foragers and gardeners," he explains. "Most of us are from the area and we all teach each other about what we've found. We're trying to do something different."

As Thoreau once wrote, "Each humblest plant, or weed, as we call it, stands there to express some thought or mood of ours." In the spring, the team gathers tender spruce shoots, which are dried and powdered to use year round. "The spruce tips have a fruity aroma, similar to rosemary," says Wolf. From down along the banks of the St. Lawrence River where it meets the coast of Gaspésie come sea rocket blossoms, an edible flower that tastes like mustard, and the plant's spicy berries, which are brined. In order to stock up on rich, dark birch syrup and vinegar, the kitchen team will tap one hundred trees at Manoir Hovey this year. "Maple is less inspiring," says the chef. "Birch syrup is dark and caramelized. It tastes a bit like molasses, but with a hint of acid at the finish." In order to heighten the effect of his inventiveness, however, Wolf keeps his presentation spare. "For most people these are all new flavors and ingredients, so we like to keep the recipes simple in order to showcase the new tastes," he explains.

The autumn celebration begins with swordfish cru, served with flavorful pine mushrooms and sea lettuce. Next come heirloom squash gnocchi, served in a sauce of blue cheese with mushrooms and birch-syrup-cured deer jerky. No ordinary squash, the chef himself grew this Knife River variety in his home garden, and sells the surplus in the Montreal farmers' market. "The flavor is incredible," he says. "It's so much more intense than commercial varieties."

For the main course, venison roasted on a bed of juniper branches is paired with smoked beets and romanesco, seasoned with green juniper oil, which has a "sharp taste," says Wolf, "and cooking on a bed of maple leaves or juniper branches brings out such flavor."

Not to be outdone, Wolf's vision is matched by the creative concoctions crafted by the inn's whimsical pastry chef, Kavi Jugdewo. Jugdewo's delectable chocolate cake trades traditional vanilla for sweet clover, which was foraged on site, dried and mixed into the batter. "It just gives a faint, sweet taste," he says. "Red clover is quite unique, with a flavor a bit like star anise, and a little like fennel seed, but sweeter." (This plays well off the Mouzette, a frothy fresh-sage-and-peach-scented cocktail by the house mixologist.)

But his pièce de résistance is an edible forest sweetscape with mock meringue mushrooms sprouting from a floor of chocolate crumble, and surrounded by edible white-chocolate-dipped lichen, which had been cooked down in elderflower syrup to remove any bitterness. "I like to play with the guests' minds a bit," Jugdewo admits. "The shape of the lichen is so beautiful. You just cannot build something like that." It's the perfect finish to a meal full of intrigue, surprise, and discovery, one that can change the very parameters of what local food means.

Something as simple as transporting an attractive indoor dining table outdoors makes a big impact, conjuring a little magic, offering guests a fresh perspective, and buoying the evening along. The menu was just as full of surprises, incorporating curious ingredients such as juniper oil, birch syrup, powdered sea lettuce, and powdered spruce tips, all of which brought the local terroir right to the palate. "For most people these are all new flavors, so we like to keep the recipes simple in order to showcase the tastes," says chef Francis Wolf.

MOUZETTE

Manoir Hovey mixologist Warren Long was inspired by a frothy dessert called mouzette to make this frothy, refreshing cocktail.

MAKES 1 COCKTAIL

4 to 6 fresh sage leaves, plus more for garnish
Pinch of sugar
2 ounces gin
2 ounces pear nectar (see Note)
1/2 ounce fresh lime juice
1 large egg white

In a cocktail shaker, muddle the sage leaves and sugar. Add the gin, pear nectar, lime juice, and egg white. Shake without ice for a minute. The egg white should create a froth. Add ice and shake again. Strain into a cocktail glass and garnish with fresh sage.

Note: To make pear nectar, simmer diced pear in a small amount of water with a star anise until tender. Remove the star anise and puree. Thin with a little water if needed. Season with salt.

Caramelized Apples The long stems on Manoir Hovey's simple caramel apples make them ripe for picking: Cook 2/3 cup sugar and 1/4 cup water in a heavy pot until an amber-colored caramel. Immediately place the pot in an ice water bath to stop the caramel from cooking. Remove the pot from the ice water bath and carefully dip 6 apples halfway into the caramel. Place the apples on a parchment paper–lined baking sheet and let dry.

SWORDFISH CRU WITH PINE MUSHROOMS, CELTUCE, AND SEA LETTUCE

This dish represents the change between summer and autumn. The swordfish Manoir Hovey sources is from Nova Scotia and is totally sustainable. Celtuce is a cultivar of lettuce, grown primarily for its thick stem. Camelina oil tastes like a blend of sunflower and colza oil.

MAKES 4 TO 6 SERVINGS

Swordfish Cru
3 tablespoons organic apple cider vinegar
1 small lovage plant (root, stem, and leaf), cleaned
6 ounces sushi-grade swordfish, sliced paper thin
1 tablespoon camelina oil
Kosher salt

Pine Mushrooms and Vegetable Reduction
1 pound pine mushrooms (also called matsutake)
2 tablespoons vegetable oil
4 to 6 carrots, diced
2 large onions, diced
1 celery rib, diced
1 pound white button mushrooms, trimmed and diced
1 kombu strip
¼ cup organic apple cider vinegar
1 teaspoon sugar

Celtuce
2 to 3 heads celtuce (also called celery lettuce and Chinese lettuce)
2 tablespoons vegetable oil
3 tablespoons fresh lemon balm leaf, blanched

Sea Lettuce Gel
1 tablespoon sea lettuce powder
1 cup spinach, blanched and drained
½ teaspoon xanthan gum
Kosher salt

For the swordfish: Gently heat the cider vinegar and pour over the lovage in a small bowl. Let cool and infuse for 2 hours. Strain.

Five minutes before serving, combine the swordfish, 2 tablespoons of the lovage vinegar, and the camelina oil, and season with salt.

For the mushrooms and reduction: Clean the pine mushrooms. Remove the stems and shave with a vegetable peeler; reserve for the final plating. Remove the gills and save for the vegetable reduction. Quarter each pine mushroom and set aside.

In a pot, heat the vegetable oil over high heat. Add the carrots, onions, celery, and half of the white button mushrooms and cook until lightly browned. Add 3 quarts water, the pine mushroom gills, and the kombu strip. Let simmer for 2 hours, then strain through a fine sieve. Transfer to a saucepan and simmer to reduce to a thick syrup, about 90 minutes. Set the vegetable reduction aside.

In a pot, combine half of the quartered pine mushrooms with 1 quart water and the remaining button mushrooms. Let simmer until fully cooked, about 10 minutes. Puree with a high-speed blender. Let the puree cool, then spread on a Silpat baking sheet. Dehydrate in the oven at 125°F, or the lowest possible setting, until crispy, 5 to 6 hours, depending on the thickness.

In a small saucepan, gently heat the cider vinegar with the sugar, then add 1 ounce of the dried pine mushroom. Let infuse for 30 minutes. Strain the mushroom vinegar.

Pour 2 tablespoons of the mushroom vinegar over the remaining quartered fresh pine mushrooms. Let sit for no more than 12 hours. Before serving, remove the pickled mushrooms from the vinegar and pat dry.

For the celtuce: Peel and blanch the celtuce stems. (Save the leaves for another use.) Cut into 2-inch pieces.

Heat the vegetable oil to 100°F in a small saucepan and blend in the blanched lemon balm. Pass the flavored oil through a fine sieve. Before serving, season the celtuce with 1 tablespoon of the lemon balm oil and season with salt.

For the sea lettuce: Blend the sea lettuce powder with the spinach and xanthan gum. Adjust the texture with about 1 tablespoon water to get a "gel." Strain through a fine sieve.

To plate: On a plate, arrange slices of the cru swordfish, then the celtuce pieces. Add the pickled pine mushrooms and pine mushroom shavings. Finish the plating with dots of the vegetable reduction and sea lettuce "gel."

RED DEER LOIN WITH BEETS, ONION REDUCTION, ROMANESCO, AND SEA ROCKET BERRIES

Autumn, the opening of deer hunting season, is also time for onions, beets, and the Brassicaceae family: broccoli, cabbage, mustard, and horseradish. Sea rocket berries, also a Brassicaceae, taste like horseradish/wasabi/mustard. Manoir Hovey likes to preserve them for year-round use. Chef Francis Wolf cooks his root vegetables on a bed of hay instead of salt—he gets the hay from a local farmer at no charge; if you don't have access to a local farmer's hay, roast the beets on a bed of salt.

MAKES 4 TO 6 SERVINGS

Brined Sea Rocket Berries

1½ tablespoons kosher salt
Sea rocket berries

Smoked Beet Puree

2 handfuls of hay
1 pound red beets
Juniper branch
Kosher salt

Baby Beets

12 baby beets
1 handful of hay

Onion Reduction

1 tablespoon vegetable oil
1 pound onions, sliced
1 celery rib, diced
2 garlic cloves, halved
1 (12-ounce) bottle dark beer

Pureed Onions

2 tablespoons unsalted butter
2 pounds onions, sliced

Romanesco and Green Juniper Oil

1 small head Romanesco broccoli, cleaned, florets separated
¼ cup vegetable oil
1 tablespoon unripe juniper berries, blanched three times

Red Deer

1 tablespoon clarified butter or vegetable oil
1 pound red deer loin, cleaned
Juniper branch
Kosher salt

To Plate

1½ teaspoons salted butter

To brine the berries: Combine 2 cups water and the salt and bring to a boil. Pour over the sea rocket berries. Cover and refrigerate for at least 15 days, or up to 1 year.

For the smoked beet puree: Preheat the oven to 275°F. In a Dutch oven, combine the hay with 1 cup water and top with the beets. Cover and bake until the beets are fully cooked, 60 to 90 minutes, depending on the size. Set up a smoker with the juniper branch. Lightly smoke the beets for about 10 minutes. Puree the beets in a high-speed blender. Season puree with salt.

For the baby beets: In a Dutch oven, cook the beets over the hay in the same way as above for 30 to 45 minutes, depending on the size of the beets. Peel and reserve.

For the onion reduction: Heat the vegetable oil in a Dutch oven over medium-high heat. Add the onions and cook until browned, about 15 minutes. Add the celery, garlic, beer, and 2 quarts water. Simmer, uncovered, for 4 hours. Strain; discard the solids. Return the onion broth to the pot and cook until reduced to a thick syrupy consistency, about 1 hour.

For the pureed onions: Melt the butter in a large pot over medium heat. Add the onions and cook until browned, about 20 minutes. Add 2 cups water and cook until almost dry, about 15 minutes. Add another 2 cups water and cook until there's no water left, 15 to 20 minutes. Puree in a high-speed blender.

For the Romanesco and juniper oil: Blanch the Romanesco in a large pot of salted water for 2 to 3 minutes. Drain and set aside. Blend the vegetable oil with the blanched juniper berries. Strain and set aside.

For the red deer: Preheat the oven to 350°F. Heat the clarified butter in a medium ovenproof skillet over medium-high heat. Add the loin and cook, turning, until browned all over. Put the juniper branch in the skillet and top with the loin. Roast in the oven until medium-rare, 7 to 10 minutes. Let rest for 3 to 5 minutes. Cut into medallions just before serving.

To plate: In a small sauté pan, heat 1 teaspoon of the butter and sauté the baby beets until hot, 3 to 4 minutes. Reheat the onion puree. Sauté the Romanesco florets in the remaining ½ teaspoon butter in a small sauté pan, then toss with 1 tablespoon of the juniper oil. Spoon the onion reduction onto each of 4 plates and top with a red deer medallion. Surround the deer with smoked beet puree, baby beets, and Romanesco. Dot with the onion puree and garnish with the sea rocket berries.

MANOIR HOVEY'S CHOCOLATE LANDSCAPE

Manoir Hovey's pastry chef, Kavi Jugdewo, created a whimsical chocolate forest with dark chocolate cake "rocks," elderflower-flavored "lichen," and meringue mushrooms nestled among chocolate crumb "dirt." If you can't forage your own lichen, simply add a few more herbs or flowers.

MAKES 6 SERVINGS

Chocolate Cake "Rocks" and "Dirt"
3 large eggs
150 grams sugar
90 grams chocolate, melted
90 grams unsalted butter, melted
50 grams all-purpose flour, sifted

Meringue Mushrooms
50 grams large egg whites
50 grams granulated sugar
50 grams confectioners' sugar
5 grams dried mushrooms, ground into a powder
Melted chocolate

Lichen (optional)
6 pieces of lichen (5 grams each)
Elderflower-flavored simple syrup
100 grams white chocolate
30 grams cocoa butter

To Assemble
Fresh herbs
Edible flowers

For the rocks and dirt: Preheat the oven to 350°F.

In a stand mixer with a whisk attachment, whip the eggs and sugar on high speed until light and fluffy. Mix together the melted chocolate and butter, then add slowly to the egg mixture. Slowly add the flour and mix until smooth. Set aside a few spoonfuls of the batter for the crumbs.

For the rocks, shape 6 pieces of aluminum foil, approximately 8 by 8 inches, into free-form bowllike shapes. These will be the molds for the cakes. Spray the foil generously with nonstick cooking spray and place in ramekins. Scoop the batter into the molds to fill two-thirds full. Bake for 10 to 12 minutes, until the cake is dry and spongy to the touch. Let cool, then peel the aluminum foil off the cakes. Store in an airtight container in the refrigerator for up to 1 week.

For the dirt crumbs, spread the remaining batter thinly on a baking sheet lined with parchment paper. Bake for about 5 minutes, until dry and spongy to the touch. Let cool, then grind to make the crumbs. Store in the refrigerator for up to 1 week.

For the meringue mushrooms: Preheat the oven to 125°F, or the lowest possible setting. Line a baking sheet with parchment paper.

In a stand mixer with the whisk attachment, whip the egg whites at high speed while gradually adding the granulated sugar until soft peaks form. Mix together the confectioners' sugar with the mushroom powder and fold into the meringue.

Pipe the meringue into mushroom shapes, about 24 domes and stems, onto the baking sheet. Bake for 8 to 10 hours, until crispy. Stick the top and the bottom parts of the meringues together with some melted chocolate. Reserve in an airtight container for up to 3 weeks.

If including lichen: Blanch the lichen in hot water for 30 seconds, then place in the elderflower-flavored simple syrup and let soak for about 10 minutes. Take the lichen out of the syrup and place on a baking sheet lined with paper towels to soak up the excess elderflower syrup.

Melt the white chocolate with the cocoa butter in the microwave until smooth. With a pastry brush, coat the blanched lichen with the white chocolate mixture. Let set in the refrigerator, then store in an airtight container for up to 3 weeks.

To assemble: For each landscape, spread cake crumbs evenly on a tray for the dirt. Place a cake rock in the dirt and surround it with the mushrooms and lichen. Finish with herbs and edible flowers to make it look as natural as possible.

Wilderness Adventure CELEBRATION

ARRIVING ON HORSEBACK, GUESTS EXPERIENCE THE ULTIMATE IN A
TRAILSIDE MEAL WITH STEAMING HOT DELICACIES SERVED IN A METICULOUSLY
CRAFTED SETTING SPARKLING WITH NATURAL GRANDEUR.

Willow Creek Cocktail*   *Yule Mule Cocktail**   *Bone Broth Consommé*
Bone Marrow with Horseradish Vinaigrette   *Fingerling Potatoes with Bacon and Truffle Mayonnaise*
Dungeness Crab Salad   *Crisp Potato Skins with Quail Eggs, Kale Chips, and Gribiche**
Cast-Iron Caramelized Parsnips and Brussels Sprouts*   *Lamb Stew**

* RECIPE PROVIDED

H ad Captain Meriwether Lewis and Lieutenant William Clark, better known as Lewis and Clark, come across such a divinely decadent trailside meal while traversing these majestic snowfields, the intrepid pair might have assumed that The Ranch at Rock Creek was itself some sort of arctic mirage. When the explorers made their way through wild Montana in 1805, commissioned by President Thomas Jefferson to seek pathways to the Pacific, they traveled with a heavy store of cornmeal, flour, sugar, and a lard-and-deer-tallow blend called "voyagers grease," and they hunted for the rest, roasting every kind of meat they came upon, from bear to prairie dog. (From time to time, Lewis liked to treat the team to his buffalo suet dumplings.) But at Rock Creek, while indulging guests with every possible luxury, and softening all the rough edges, a devotion to the land and its history keeps Montana's invigorating frontier spirit alive.

Sprawling over six thousand stunning acres outside of Philipsburg, The Ranch at Rock Creek was originally a mining claim, back when the silver boom was on and when sapphires glistened in the Rock Creek drainage. In 1888, Helena was home to more millionaires per capita than any other city in the world, and Rock Creek imparts both a sense of antique prosperity and the thrill of adventure.

"The winter here is long, and everybody is happy to get out and to get active," says chef Josh Drage. "You can't just stay holed up. You have to go out and celebrate the season." One of the best ways to work up an appetite is to saddle one of the ranch's seventy-five hundred head of horses and hit the trails. Riders make their way through the beautiful land, with a skim of ice covering the creek; by late afternoon they arrive and tie up at Trapper Cabin, a year-round canvas tent and wood cabin hybrid, and the ultimate in "glamping." A fire burns in the pit, and woolen runners soften the raw cut-fir table decked with artfully arranged vases of

A cut-fir table, designed so guests can stand—as sitting would prove too chilly—is beautifully appointed with pewter cups and candlesticks, plaid woolens, an arrangement of roses, Brussels sprouts, and pomegranates, all standing on a carpet of evergreen boughs (see previous spread). Rock Creek is known for elegantly taking the edge off guests' enjoyment of Montana's rugged wilderness.

roses, pomegranates, spruce boughs, and even Brussels sprouts peeking out from the foliage. "We built the table high so everyone could stand," says Drage. "In wintertime no one wants to sit down outside to eat—you'd just get cold."

The dinner is full of sumptuous contrasts, beginning with fireside appetizers of hot bone broth consommé served in mugs, and bone marrow with a black trumpet mushroom and horseradish vinaigrette spread onto crusty bread. "For me it all started around those bones and the fire," Drage explains. "Native Americans used to roast and crack bones on an open fire. It's so elemental and nutritious."

"The idea of this menu," he continues, "is the simplicity of the ingredients are exposed in their most elemental forms." Fire plays off ice, while local and opulent come into harmony with dishes like fingerling potatoes served with house-smoked bacon, sage, and truffle mayonnaise. "Historically, you'd trade, barter, or borrow from neighbors, and we do rely on local producers and growers," says Drage. "But we also use elements of luxury. It's great to live off the land without being held hostage to that notion." A salad of Dungeness crab and winter cress is dotted with pickled cranberries and roasted local sunchokes, all dressed in grapefruit vinaigrette. Meanwhile, Drage's witty "potatoes and eggs" means Northern Divine caviar atop a crisp potato skin, and cured char roe on a delicate kale chip, served with quail eggs and sauce gribiche.

Growing up in Alaska, the chef learned about the pleasures of Dutch oven slow-cooking, traditional to the West, from his grandmother. He offers guests caramelized carrots and Brussels sprouts with Orleans mustard dressing cooked over the fire in a cast-iron skillet, as well as individual servings of his main course, braised lamb and olive stew with mutton merguez sausage in hot cast-iron pans. The beauty of the lamb is, as the chef would say, elemental. "The stew isn't disguised," Drage notes. "It's super simple. Hearty and warm."

Served by a warming fire, Drage's version of a mule cocktail includes muddled cranberries and rosemary, while his signature trailside cocktail, the Willow Creek, blends Whyte Laydie gin from nearby Montgomery Distillery with grapefruit and cranberry juices, and is served with a sprig of juniper, a plant which grows all around the campsite. "And then it's back onto the trails," he says. In a state with a density of six people per square mile, and where the elk, deer, and antelope populations outnumber humans, there is so much to see. "Coming down the trail just before arriving," Drage says, "we saw a bobcat, a bighorn sheep, and a mule deer—all on the way to dinner!"

An abundance of floral arrangements brighten the porch of the property's peacefully secluded Trapper Cabin, a canvas tent and wood cabin hybrid accommodating guests year round, with a little kitchenette and a cozy king-sized bed. Stargazing from the cabin's outdoor soaking tub is sublime. In the warmer months, guests can fly-fish in Rock Creek from the cabin's front door.

WILLOW CREEK

The Ranch at Rock Creek delivers these cocktails to guests beside the fire on the banks of Rock Creek in Granite County, Montana. The Montgomery Distillery distills its gin from juniper berries from Granite County. In fact, this particular stretch of the creek is lined with juniper trees; just beyond the warmth of the fire you can see one growing.

MAKES 1 COCKTAIL

1½ ounces Montgomery Whyte Laydie Gin
2 ounces fresh grapefruit juice
Splash of elderflower liqueur
Splash of cucumber vodka
Dash of rhubarb bitters
Splash of cranberry juice

Combine the gin, grapefruit juice, elderflower liqueur, vodka, bitters, and cranberry juice in a cocktail shaker with ice. Shake and strain into a glass.

YULE MULE

The mule has become all the rage, but in Montana, the citrusy cocktail finished with ginger beer has always been a part of everyday life. The ranch created a mule that celebrates winter's embrace with the addition of muddled cranberries and rosemary.

MAKES 1 COCKTAIL

2 cranberries
10 rosemary needles, plus a rosemary sprig for garnish
  (optional)
Splash of cranberry juice
1½ ounces Montgomery QuickSilver Vodka
Ginger beer
Sugar-coated cranberries (optional)

Muddle the cranberries and rosemary in a glass. Add the cranberry juice and vodka. Do not strain. Transfer to a copper mug filled with ice and top with ginger beer. If you like, garnish with a sprig of rosemary and sugar-coated cranberries.

CRISP POTATO SKINS WITH QUAIL EGGS, KALE CHIPS, AND GRIBICHE

At The Ranch at Rock Creek, chef Josh Drage embraces winter as a time to celebrate the outdoor extremes and delightful contrasting textures. To capture that on a plate, the ranch serves crispy potato skins with sustainable white sturgeon caviar from British Columbia and a cured char roe from the Pacific Northwest, along with a sunny-side up quail egg (a small, potent package of protein), Parmesan-dusted kale chips, and an intense gribiche sauce. Chef Drage says the dish captures the feel of winter.

MAKES 8 SERVINGS

Preserved Lemons

6 tablespoons kosher salt
4½ ounces sugar
1 pound lemons, thinly sliced

Kale Chips

½ cup grated Parmesan cheese
½ cup olive oil
1 bunch Red Russian kale
Fleur de sel and freshly cracked black pepper

Soured Cream

1 cup heavy cream
1 tablespoon buttermilk
1 teaspoon fresh lemon juice

Sauce Gribiche

6 Mission Mountain organic eggs, hard-boiled and peeled
2 tablespoons Dijon mustard
½ cup olive oil
2 pickled green tomatoes, peeled, seeded, and diced
½ bunch fresh parsley sprigs, chopped
1 tablespoon capers, chopped
1 tablespoon chopped fresh chives
Cayenne pepper sauce
Kosher salt

Crisp Potato Skins

3 or 4 medium Yukon gold potatoes
Canola oil for frying
Fleur de sel

To Plate

Northern Divine sturgeon caviar
Fleur de sel–cured char roe
Calabrian chili oil
8 Montana quail eggs, cooked sunny-side up
Fleur de sel

For the preserved lemons: Mix together the kosher salt and sugar. Shingle the lemon slices in a broad square glass dish, heavily sprinkling the salt and sugar mixture in between each layer and ensuring full contact of the curing salt with the lemon slices. Wrap the glass container in plastic wrap and set out at room temperature for 1 week. Then move to the refrigerator, where the preserved lemons will keep for 2 to 4 weeks. Rinse before use.

For the kale chips: Preheat the oven to 325°F. Blend the Parmesan and olive oil in a blender. Transfer to a small bowl. Remove the center rib from each large leaf of kale. Lay out the leaves and brush on the Parmesan-oil mixture, evenly covering the tops. Arrange the leaves flat on a baking sheet, leaving some space in between each one. Season with sea salt and cracked pepper. Bake for about 10 minutes, until crisp but not too brown. Let cool. The chips can be served right away or stored for a few days in a plastic bag.

To sour the cream: In a mason jar, combine the cream, buttermilk, and lemon juice. Cover with a kitchen towel secured with a rubber band. Let sit overnight at room temperature. Refrigerate until ready to serve.

For the Sauce Gribiche: Separate the egg whites from the yolks. Chop the egg whites and set aside. Place the yolks in a mortar and add the mustard. Begin to work it with a pestle, slowly adding the olive oil and working until you get a smooth paste.

In a small bowl, combine the egg whites, yolk mixture, green tomatoes, parsley, capers, and chives and mix thoroughly. Season with cayenne pepper sauce and a pinch of kosher salt.

For the potato skins: Preheat the oven to 400°F. Bake the potatoes for 40 minutes, or until soft when poked with a knife. Heat 1 inch of canola oil in a cast-iron pan to 325°F. Halve the baked potatoes and scoop out the flesh, leaving a scant bit on the skin, then tear each potato skin once or twice more. (Save the remaining potato flesh for another use. In the ranch's kitchen the skins were a by-product of making gnocchi, so the kitchen found a use for them with this recipe.) Add the potato skins to the hot oil and fry until golden, about 2 minutes. Hit them with a touch of sea salt as soon as you pull them from the oil.

To plate: Have fun plating this dish. Use the potato skins and kale chips as vehicles for the caviar and the roe. Make sure the soured cream is on the caviar, and the Calabrian chili oil is nearby. Put a spoonful of gribiche on the plate for additional scooping. Sprinkle the quail egg with a bit of fleur de sel. Peel away the flesh of the preserved lemon with a spoon, leaving the cured rind. Rinse with water and place on the plate near the gribiche.

CAST-IRON CARAMELIZED PARSNIPS AND BRUSSELS SPROUTS

The cast-iron pan, the hallmark of a Western kitchen, has the ability to hold and distribute heat evenly, making it the perfect pan for caramelizing vegetables. In the winter, The Ranch at Rock Creek selects grown-in-Montana parsnips and Brussels sprouts; both have a wonderful relationship with the earthy whole grain mustard dressing.

MAKES 8 SERVINGS

Orleans Mustard Dressing

1 cup mayonnaise
3 tablespoons whole grain mustard
1 to 2 tablespoons sherry vinegar
1/2 teaspoon fresh thyme leaves
1/4 teaspoon freshly cracked black pepper
Sea salt

Parsnips and Sprouts

6 parsnips, peeled
1 pound whole Brussels sprouts
2 tablespoons unsalted butter
6 fresh thyme sprigs
Kosher salt and freshly cracked black pepper

For the dressing: Stir together the mayonnaise, mustard, sherry vinegar, thyme, pepper, and sea salt. Cover and refrigerate until use.

For the parsnips and sprouts: Cut the parsnips lengthwise into long quarters. Trim off the cut end of each Brussels sprout and peel off any loose outer leaves.

Heat a large cast-iron pan over medium-high heat. Add 1 tablespoon of the butter and, as it is melting, which should happen quickly, add the parsnips. Use the initial heat of the pan to begin the caramelizing. Once the color develops, add the thyme sprigs. Turn the heat down to medium-low to finish cooking, until the parsnips deepen in color, about 10 minutes. (Chef Drage likes the vegetables to still have a bite to them, so he caramelizes them quickly.) Remove from the pan and spread out on a baking sheet to cool down. Remove and discard the thyme sprigs.

Repeat with the remaining 1 tablespoon butter and the sprouts, cooking them for about 10 minutes, until crisp and tender.

To serve: Combine the vegetables in a cast-iron pan, season with kosher salt and pepper, and keep warm by the fire. Place the dressing in a small decorative bowl to use as a dip.

LAMB STEW

Chef Josh Drage combines the light, delicate meat from a leg of Willow Spring Ranch organic lamb with their merguez mutton sausage for a simple stew that is well balanced and warming.

MAKES 6 TO 8 SERVINGS

Lamb

1 tablespoon olive oil
2 yellow onions, quartered
2 large carrots, cut into large pieces
1 leek, trimmed, halved lengthwise, washed well between layers, and halved crosswise
5 garlic cloves
3 bay leaves
1 (2- to 4-pound) bone-in leg of lamb
2 cups beef stock
1 cup dry red wine

To Finish

4 tablespoons (½ stick) unsalted butter
½ pound merguez mutton sausage, thickly sliced and the casings peeled off
3 shallots, diced
1 leek, trimmed, halved lengthwise, washed well between layers, and diced
⅔ cup all-purpose flour
½ cup pitted kalamata olives
2 tablespoons sherry vinegar
1 small bundle (about 12 sprigs) fresh thyme, tied
Kosher salt and freshly ground black pepper

For the lamb: Preheat the oven to 250°F.

Heat a Dutch oven over medium heat and add the olive oil. Add the onions, carrots, leek, garlic, and bay leaves and cook for about 1 minute. (There's no need to cook the vegetables through.) Add the lamb to the pot along with the stock and red wine. Cover the pot, transfer to the oven, and bake for 3 hours.

Increase the heat to 325°F, uncover, and continue to bake for 20 minutes, until the leg is nicely browned on the top. Turn the leg back into the liquid and allow the top to brown again, about 20 minutes. Repeat the process, developing flavor in the broth until the meat falls off the bone when tugged at, 60 to 90 minutes total (after the initial 3-hour braise). Remove the leg from the liquid and let cool.

Strain the cooking liquid and remove the fat. Pick the meat from the bone and remove any unwanted parts. At this stage the meat should be in nice 3- or 4-ounce pieces with no bones. (The stock and meat can be combined and stored in the refrigerator for up to 5 days.)

To finish the stew: Warm the Dutch oven over medium heat. Add 2 tablespoons of the butter and the sausage and cook until browned; remove with a slotted spoon to a paper towel–lined plate. Add the remaining 2 tablespoons butter and the diced shallots and leek to the pot and cook until warmed through. Sprinkle in the flour and cook, stirring, for about 12 minutes to create a roux. Add the strained cooking stock, whisking it into the roux until a uniform consistency. Reduce the heat and add the olives, sherry vinegar, and thyme. Add the braised lamb and merguez to the stew and season with salt and pepper. Cover and finish at a simmer for 30 to 45 minutes. Remove the thyme, taste the stew one more time, and adjust the seasoning if necessary.

New Year's Eve PARTY

IN THE BERKSHIRES, A VIBRANT AND EXTRAVAGANT GILDED AGE CASTLE-CUM-"COTTAGE" LEAPS TO LIFE WITH A GRACIOUS, GLAMOROUS FORMAL DINNER TO USHER IN THE NEW YEAR.

———

Champagne   Virgin Grapefruit Mojito   Ginger Lime Martini*   Orange Creamsicle**
*Buckwheat Blini with Caviar and Sour Cream**
*Rohan Duck Breasts with Parsnip Puree, Brussels Sprouts, and Kaffir Lime Jus**

*RECIPE PROVIDED

A t Blantyre, the Gilded Age castle–cum–Berkshires "cottage" luxury is carefully tempered with elegance, a delicate balance that American author and society doyenne Edith Wharton once called "the complex art of civilized living." As every good host or hostess knows, the trick is in making it all look easy.

On New Year's Eve at Blantyre, the festivities began with buckwheat blinis and caviar and a flurry of mocktails, building momentum through an exquisite seven-course tasting menu, which included Katama Bay oysters and Rohan Duck Breasts with Parsnip Puree, Brussels Sprouts, and Kaffir Lime Jus, and hitting the heights at the stroke of midnight, when guests merrily rang in the New Year with a magnum of Cristal Rosé 2006, and as the band played "I've Got the World on a String." It was a night to remember, and one that the Gilded Age revelers who once graced Blantyre's gracious halls would have loved, right down to the early morning root-vegetable bisque, served with sandwiches.

Decked with towers, turrets, and gargoyles, Blantyre was built in 1902 by turn-of-the-century entrepreneur Robert Warden Paterson, inspired by his ancestral Scotland. Like the era's other larger-than-life hosts, Paterson and his wife, Marie Louise, came to summer in Lenox, Massachusetts, from New York, taking in the fresh air and indulging deeply in the area's pastoral pleasures. The Berkshires were less formal than Newport, less antic than Bar Harbor, and were utterly fashionable between 1870 and 1915.

Just a mile away, during the same year that Blantyre was constructed, Wharton built The Mount, her beloved country idyll. "The Mount was to give me country cares and joys, long happy drives through wooded lanes of that loveliest region," she wrote, "the companionship

Ann Fitzpatrick, who poured her passion into Blantyre's every detail and who passed away in 2016, said of the place, "Our guests know once they arrive in the driveway that their cares will drift away." When she became owner of the property in 1981, Fitzpatrick painstakingly re-created its former grandeur—restoring everything but the tin suit of armor that once stood in the main hall.

of a few dear friends, and the freedom from trivial obligations. . . . " The Vanderbilt clan reigned nearby at Elm Court, with its 106 rooms. A stone's throw away, steel magnate Andrew Carnegie, a favorite Blantyre guest, whiled away his summers at Shadowbrook, briefly known as America's largest private residence. At Bellefontaine, modeled after Marie Antoinette's Petit Trianon, 1,800 European marble statues graced the formal gardens.

Employing three hundred, including a full-time gardening staff to oversee its nine connecting greenhouses, which provided out-of-season peaches and grapes as well as masses of flowers, Blantyre was just as sumptuous. Avid world travelers, the Patersons displayed their collected treasures at Blantyre—exotic Chinese jades and lacquered chests, French fans, and Belgian tapestries—but the backdrop was purely British, right down to a collection of Gainsborough portraits that hung on its walls.

Too soon, however, the reality of the newly established income tax caught up with the most vibrant Gilded Age barons, including Paterson. By 1980, when Jack and Jane Fitzpatrick bought the property for their daughter Ann, Blantyre had passed through several foreclosures and had been utterly stripped of its charm. Ann took on the formidable challenge of resurrecting Blantyre's distant glory, and, after much hard work, the house now boasts the easeful opulence of its roots. Everything but the tin suit of armor that once stood in the Main Hall has been restored, the owners having scoured antiques markets and auctions worldwide for the perfect Tiffany lamp to brighten up the music room, a Dresden chandelier to hang over the breakfast table, the antique china on which to serve Blantyre's haute-homey fare, and its tufted sofas, all of which perfectly exude serene English grandeur. As one writer put it recently, the Blantyre experience means "luxury tempered by good taste."

Since 2005, Blantyre has been open year round, offering classical wintertime diversions such as snowshoeing and cross-country skiing, ice skating, and hot chocolate with homemade marshmallows. Embarking on a New Year's Day sleigh ride is a well-loved house tradition, a happy outing for all the weekend's guests—except two, who preferred to pass a secluded weekend alone in their room. (We can only imagine what Wharton would think.) But whether donning a tiara to join in the fun, or retreating into the cozy depths, Blantyre is part of a gentler time.

A wonderful proliferation of layers brings richness to the party setting, especially during the holidays, when a touch or two of gold imparts a burnished glow. On a sleek marquetry sidebar at Blantyre, gold-rimmed antique Dresden china is ever at the ready for the next great party.

Utterly in keeping with the historic grandeur of the house, every object found there seems to boast a storied past. The table setting is Dresden china. Crimson tulips elegantly arch from an antique silver wine bucket, purchased at an estate sale, and an early twentieth-century French chandelier sparkles above a bust carved by artist Daniel Chester French, who worked in the area and also created the Lincoln Memorial. The champagne coups are crystal, by London's William Yeoward, purveyor to Prince Charles.

BLANTYRE MOCKTAILS

Champagne is the drink of choice at Blantyre's New Year's Eve gala, but Blantyre's offering of festive alcohol-free cocktails ensures that everyone can join in the celebration and a toast at the strike of midnight.

Virgin Grapefruit Mojito

MAKES 1 COCKTAIL

8 ounces fresh grapefruit juice
1 soupspoon honey
Splash of club soda
Grapefruit wedge
Fresh mint sprig (optional)

Fill a glass with ice cubes. Pour the grapefruit juice into a shaker and add the honey. Shake and pour into the ice-filled glass. Finish with a splash of club soda. Garnish with a grapefruit wedge and fresh mint, if available.

Ginger Lime Martini

MAKES 1 COCKTAIL

3 ounces agave margarita juice or fresh juice from 2 limes
2 ounces ginger ale
Lime wedge

Pour the juice and ginger ale into a frozen martini glass. Garnish with a wedge of lime.

Orange Creamsicle

MAKES 1 COCKTAIL

3 ounces fresh orange juice
2 dashes of pure vanilla extract
Club soda
Orange slice

Fill a glass with ice cubes. Mix together the orange juice and vanilla. Pour into the glass and finish with club soda. Garnish with a slice of orange.

BUCKWHEAT BLINI WITH CAVIAR AND SOUR CREAM

Blantyre's yeast-based pancakes are the perfect bed for caviar resting on a pillow of sour cream. Another decadent way to enjoy blini: with thin slices of silky smoked salmon.

MAKES 12 SERVINGS

1 cup plus 2 tablespoons whole milk
¾ cup heavy cream
¾ cup buckwheat flour
¾ cup bread flour
¾ teaspoon dry yeast
3 large eggs, separated
2 tablespoons sugar
2 teaspoons kosher salt
About 2 tablespoons canola oil
Sour cream
Caviar
Chopped fresh chives

In a small bowl, mix the milk and cream together. In a good-size bowl, mix together the buckwheat flour and bread flour, and add the yeast. Make a well in the dry ingredients and stir in the milk mixture, the 3 egg yolks, and sugar. Whisk gently to make a lump-free batter. Stir in the salt. Cover the bowl with plastic wrap and let the batter rise for 2 hours in a warm place (at least room temperature).

In another bowl, whip the 3 egg whites to soft peaks, then fold into the batter.

Heat a large skillet over medium heat. Add a film of canola oil. When the oil is hot, ladle in portions of about 2 tablespoons batter to make small pancakes. Cook until bubbles begin to form on the top and the edges start to turn golden. Flip and cook on the other side until golden brown. Repeat with additional oil and the remaining batter. The blini can be made up to 2 days ahead and stored in the refrigerator, covered.

To serve: Arrange the blini in one layer on baking sheets and reheat in a 350°F oven until warmed through. Top each blini with a dollop of sour cream and caviar, then garnish with chives.

ROHAN DUCK BREASTS WITH PARSNIP PUREE, BRUSSELS SPROUTS, AND KAFFIR LIME JUS

Blantyre's New Year's duck breasts feature ingredients that are colorful, seasonal, and flavorful. The richness of the duck, the sweetness of the parsnips, the earthiness of the sprouts, and the bright acidity of the kaffir lime combine for an elegant entrée truly worthy of the special evening.

MAKES 4 SERVINGS

1 pound parsnips, peeled and cut into uniform chunks
3 tablespoons unsalted butter, plus more for the Brussels sprouts
Kosher salt and freshly ground black pepper
2 cups Brussels sprouts, outer leaves trimmed and sprouts
  cut in half
3/4 cup veal stock
1 kaffir lime leaf (available in specialty stores)
2 tablespoons canola oil
4 (6- to 7-ounce) duck breasts

In a large skillet, combine the parsnips, butter, salt and pepper, and enough water to just barely cover the parsnips. Bring to a simmer and cook until easily pierced with a knife, about 12 minutes. Drain and reserve 1/2 cup of the cooking water. Puree in a food processor with the reserved cooking water.

Blanch the Brussels sprouts in a large pot of salted water for 4 to 5 minutes, just until tender (pierce with the tip of a knife to check). Shock in ice water to stop the cooking. Drain.

Simmer the stock with the lime leaf for 5 minutes. Discard the lime leaf.

Heat the canola oil in a large skillet over medium-high heat. Add the duck breasts, skin side down, and cook until seared. Reduce the heat and cook for 6 minutes, then turn over the breasts and cook for another 2 minutes for medium-rare. Remove from the heat and let rest for at least 5 minutes before slicing.

To plate: Sizzle the blanched Brussels sprout halves in butter in a skillet. Warm the parsnip puree and the lime jus. On each of 4 plates, arrange a quenelle of parsnip puree, a few Brussels sprout halves, and duck slices, then drizzle jus over all.

What goes better with black tie than a glittering tiara or a crown? In the afternoon, the staff laid out a sparkling selection of regal headwear for guests to choose from, setting the evening's lightheartedly decadent tone. Over eight hundred tutti-frutti balloons, each trailing its shimmering ribbon, cast a delightful spell in the stately halls, and at midnight, the swing band played "I've Got the World on a String."

RECIPE INDEX

ACKNOWLEDGMENTS

THIS BOOK COULD NOT have come to life without the help and assistance of Charles Miers, the publisher of Rizzoli, who embraced the project at the outset and recognized the uniqueness of such a collaboration. Seventeen individually owned Relais & Châteaux properties worked in harmony with Sandy Gilbert Freidus, Rizzoli senior editor, who curated and organized the effort with her unfailing eye for detail.

Paul Roelofs, the book's inspired creative director and designer, crafted a stunning, virtual tour of these stylish and elegant North American Relais hideaways.

Writer Jessica Kerwin Jenkins narrated this colorful journey with panache, while revealing the secrets of these imaginative and passionate hosts.

Brenda Homick, the director of member services for Relais & Châteaux North America, played an instrumental role in the book's success by coordinating the multifaceted project. Daniel Hostettler, treasurer of Relais & Châteaux North America and general manager of Ocean House, helped organize and facilitate the participating members.

Photographers Melanie Acevedo and David Engelhardt captured the beauty and magic of these exotic sanctuaries.

Hilary Ney managed the task of writing refinement, while Elizabeth Smith served as copyeditor. Special thanks to Deri Reed, recipe editor, and Deborah Weiss Geline, recipe copyeditor.

This book celebrates the unique soul and spirit of the wonderful North American Relais & Châteaux properties—in particular the seventeen featured within. We thank them for inviting us into their private worlds and sharing their entertaining secrets.

Patrick O'Connell

Chef Proprietor
The Inn at Little Washington
President, Relais & Châteaux North America

Secluded behind high walls, a profusion of blooms and antique curiosities fill the meandering garden at The Charlotte Inn, in Edgartown, Martha's Vineyard, intriguing guests at every turn.

RELAIS & CHATEAUX

NORTH AMERICA

CANADA

Auberge Saint-Antoine
8 rue Saint-Antoine
Québec, QC
G1K 4C9
888.692.2211

**Clayoquot
Wilderness Resort**
P.O. Box 130
Tofino, BC
V0R 2Z0
250.266.0397

**Hastings House
Country House Hotel**
160 Upper Ganges Road
Salt Spring Island, BC
V8K 2S2
250.537.2362

Kensington Riverside Inn
1126 Memorial Drive,
Northwest
Calgary, AB
T2N 3E3
403.228.4442

**Langdon Hall Country
House**
1 Langdon Drive
Cambridge, ON
N3H 4R8
519.740.2100

Manoir Hovey
575 Hovey Road
North Hatley, QC
J0B 2C0
819.842.2421

Post Hotel & Spa
200 Pipestone Road
Lake Louise, AB
T0L 1E0
403.522.3989

Restaurant Europea
1227 rue de la Montagne
Montréal, QC
H3G 1Z2
514.398.9229

Restaurant Initiale
54 rue Saint-Pierre
Québec, QC
G1K 4A1
418.694.1818

Sonora Resort
4580 Cowley Crescent
Richmond, BC
V7B 7B8
604.233.0460

Toqué! Restaurant
900 Place
Jean-Paul-Riopelle
Montréal, QC
H2Z 2B2
514.499.2084

Wedgewood Hotel & Spa
845 Hornby Street
Vancouver, BC
V6Z 1V1
604.689.7777

Wickaninnish Inn
Osprey Lane at
Chesterman Beach
Tofino, BC
V0R 2Z0
250.725.3100

CARIBBEAN

Cobblers Cove
Road View
Speightstown
St. Peter, Barbados
+1.246.422.2291

Eden Roc at Cap Cana
Cap Cana
Juanillo, Playa Bavaro
23000
Dominican Republic
+1.809.469.7469

Eden Rock - St Barths
St. Jean Bay
Saint Barthélemy
F97133
French West Indies
+590.590.29.79.99

Hôtel Le Toiny
Anse de Toiny
Saint Barthélemy
F97133
French West Indies
+590.590.27.88.88

**Montpelier
Plantation & Beach**
P.O. Box 474
Charlestown
Nevis, West Indies
+1.869.469.3462

MEXICO

**Esperanza, An Auberge
Resort**
Carretera Transpeninsular
Km 7 Manzana 10
Punta Ballena
Cabo San Lucas
Baja California Sur
23410
Mexico
+52.624.145.6400

Hotel Solar de las Ánimas
Calle Ramón Corona #86,
Colonia Centro
Tequila, Jalisco
46400
Mexico
+ 52.374.742.6700

Imanta Punta De Mita
Montenahuac S/N, Lote L
Higuerra Blanca,
Bahia de Banderas
Nayarit
63734
Mexico
+52.329.298.4200

**Las Mañanitas Hotel
Garden Restaurant & Spa**
Ricardo Linares 107 Centro
Cuernavaca, Morelos
62000
Mexico
+52.777.362.0000

Villa Maria Cristina
Paseo de La Presa 76
Guanajuato
36000
Mexico
+52.473.731.2182

UNITED STATES

Addison Restaurant
5200 Grand Del Mar Way
San Diego, CA
92130
858.314.1900

Auberge du Soleil
180 Rutherford Hill Road
Rutherford, CA
94573
707.963.1211

Bedford Post
954 Old Post Road
Bedford, NY
10506
914.234.7800

Blackberry Farm
1471 West Millers Cove Road
Walland, TN
37886
865.984.8166

Blantyre
16 Blantyre Road
Lenox, MA
01240
413.637.3556

Camden Harbour Inn
83 Bayview Street
Camden, ME
04843
207.236.4200

Canlis
2576 Aurora Avenue North
Seattle, WA
98109
206.283.3313

Canoe Bay
P.O. Box 28
Chetek, WI
54728
715.924.4594

Castle Hill Inn
590 Ocean Avenue
Newport, RI
02840
401.849.3800

Château du Sureau
48688 Victoria Lane
Oakhurst, CA
93644
559.683.6860

Daniel
60 East 65th Street
New York, NY
10065
212.288.0033

Del Posto
85 10th Avenue
New York, NY
10011
212.497.8090

Dunton Hot Springs
52068 Road 38
Dolores, CO
81323
970.882.4800

Eleven Madison Park
11 Madison Avenue
New York, NY
10010
212.889.0905

Everest
440 South LaSalle Street,
#4000
Chicago, IL
60605
312.663.8920

Glenmere Mansion
634 Pine Hill Road
Chester, NY
10918
845.469.1900

Established in 1954, Relais & Châteaux is an association of more than 540 landmark hotels and restaurants operated by independent innkeepers, chefs, and owners who share a passion for their businesses and a desire for authenticity in their relationships with their clientele. • Relais & Châteaux is established around the globe, from the Napa Valley vineyards and French Provence to the beaches of the Indian Ocean. It offers an introduction to a lifestyle inspired by local culture and a unique dip into human history. • Relais & Châteaux members have a driving desire to protect and promote the richness and diversity of the world's cuisine and traditions of hospitality.

Homestead Inn-Thomas Henkelmann
420 Field Point Road
Greenwich, CT
06830
203.869.7500

Hotel Fauchère
401 Broad Street
Milford, PA
18337
570.409.1212

Hotel Les Mars
27 North Street
Healdsburg, CA
95448
707.433.4211

Hôtel Saint Germain
2516 Maple Avenue
Dallas, TX
75201
214.871.2516

Hotel Wailea
555 Kaukahi Street
Wailea, HI
96753
808.874.0500

Jean Georges
1 Central Park West
New York, NY
10023
212.299.3900

Lake Placid Lodge
144 Lodge Way
Lake Placid, NY
12946
518.523.2700

L'Auberge Carmel
7th Avenue and
Monte Verde Street
Carmel-by-the-Sea, CA
93921
831.624.8578

Manresa Restaurant
320 Village Lane
Los Gatos, CA
95030
408.354.4330

Meadowood Napa Valley
900 Meadowood Lane
St. Helena, CA
94574
707.531.4788

Menton
354 Congress Street
Boston, MA
02210
617.737.0099

Ocean House
1 Bluff Avenue
Watch Hill, RI
02891
401.584.7000

Old Edwards Inn & Spa
445 Main Street
Highlands, NC
28741
828.526.9784

Per Se
10 Columbus Circle
New York, NY
10019
212.823.9335

Planters Inn
112 North Market Street
Charleston, SC
29401
843.722.2345

Quince Restaurant
470 Pacific Avenue
San Francisco, CA
94133
415.775.8500

Rancho Valencia
5921 Valencia Circle
Rancho Santa Fe, CA
92067
858.756.1123

Restaurant Gary Danko
800 North Point Street
San Francisco, CA
94109
415.749.2060

Royal Blues Hotel
45 Northeast 21st Avenue
Deerfield Beach, FL
33441
954.857.2929

Saison
178 Townsend Street
San Francisco, CA
94107
415.828.7990

The Charlotte Inn
27 South Summer Street
Edgartown, MA
02539
508.627.4151

The Fearrington House Inn, Restaurant & Spa
2000 Fearrington
Village Center
Pittsboro, NC
27312
919.542.2121

The French Laundry
6640 Washington Street
Yountville, CA
94599
707.944.2380

The Home Ranch
P.O. Box 822
Clark, CO
80428
970.879.1780

The Inn at Dos Brisas
10000 Champion Drive
Washington, TX
77880
979.277.7750

The Inn at Hastings Park
2027 Massachusetts Avenue
Lexington, MA
02421
781.301.6660

**The Inn at
Little Washington**
Middle and Main Street
Washington, VA
22747
540.675.3800

The Inn of the Five Graces
150 East De Vargas Street
Santa Fe, NM
87501
505.992.0957

The Ivy Hotel
205 East Biddle Street
Baltimore, MD
21202
443 815 1207

The Little Nell
675 East Durant Street
Aspen, CO
81611
970.920.4600

The Lodge at Glendorn
1000 Glendorn Drive
Bradford, PA
16701
814.362.6511

The Lodge at Sea Island
100 Retreat Avenue
St. Simons Island, GA
31522
912.638.3611

The Mayflower Grace
118 Woodbury Road
Washington, CT
06793
860.868.9466

The Pitcher Inn
275 Main Street
Warren, VT
05674
802.496.6350

The Point
222 Beaverwood Road
Saranac Lake, NY
12983
518.891.5674

The Ranch at Rock Creek
79 Carriage House Lane
Philipsburg, MT
59858
406.859.6027

The Surrey
20 East 76th Street
New York, NY
10021
212.905.1477

The Wauwinet
120 Wauwinet Road
Nantucket, MA
02584
508.228.8768

The White Barn Inn & Spa
37 Beach Avenue
Kennebunk Beach, ME
04043
207.967.2321

Triple Creek Ranch
5551 West Fork Road
Darby, MT
59829
406.821.4600

Twin Farms
452 Royalton Turnpike
Barnard, VT
05031
802.234.9999

Weekapaug Inn
25 Spray Rock Road
Westerly, RI
02891
401.322.0301

Westglow Resort and Spa
224 Westglow Circle
Blowing Rock, NC
28605
828.295.4463

Windham Hill Inn
311 Lawrence Drive
West Townshend, VT
05359
802.874.4080

Winvian Farm
155 Alain White Road
Morris, CT
06763
860.567.9600

Captions

Page 1

At Napa Valley's Auberge du Soleil, a mix of white scabiosa, lisianthus, green hydrangea—and the occasional artichoke—were artfully arranged among the roses which ranged from yellow garden roses, to soft peach 'Juilienne Roses' and blush Sahara.

Page 2

With an eye for detail, Theresa Henkelmann, of the Homestead Inn-Thomas Henkelmann in Greenwich, Connecticut, commissioned customized place cards from a master calligrapher to match the vivid jewel-toned floral arrangements.

Page 4

At The Fearrington House Inn, in Pittsboro, North Carolina, charming bouquets of herbs—from rosemary to thyme—clipped in the kitchen garden behind the restaurant awaken the senses with a delicious, fresh scent.

Credits

Auberge du Soleil

Design and Flowers: Rion Designs
Hair and Makeup: Carrie Aldous
Clothes and Styling: Karen Caldwell
Linens: La Tavola Fine Linen
Rentals: Classic Party Rentals
Rentals: Favor Custom Gifts
Lighting: Napa Valley Media

Glenmere Mansion

Styling: Matthew Robbins and Luis Otoya
  for Matthew Robbins Design
Invitation/Menu/Paper Accessories:
Regas Studio

First published in the United States of America in 2016
by Rizzoli International Publications, Inc.
300 Park Avenue South
New York, New York 10010
www.rizzoliusa.com

Text © 2016 Relais & Châteaux North America

Photography © 2016 by Melanie Acevedo and David Engelhardt, specifically:

Melanie Acevedo: front cover, pages 1, 6, and images for the following celebrations: The Inn at Dos Brisas, Auberge du Soleil, Glenmere Mansion, Blackberry Farm, The Inn at Little Washington, Blantyre

David Engelhardt: back cover, pages 2, 4, and images for the following celebrations: The Charlotte Inn, Ocean House, Langdon Hall Country House, Weekapaug Inn, Esperanza, an Auberge Resort, Homestead Inn-Thomas Henkelmann, Meadowood Napa Valley, Planters Inn, The Fearrington House Inn, Manoir Hovey, The Ranch at Rock Creek

Project Editor: Sandra Gilbert
Creative Direction and Design: Paul Roelofs
Production Manager: Rebecca Ambrose

2016 2017 2018 2019 / 10 9 8 7 6 5 4 3 2 1

Printed in China

ISBN-13: 978-0-8478-4931-4

Library of Congress Control Number: 2016939092